D0921327

Praise for *Dollarlogic*

Andy Martin takes a difficult subject like asset allocation and risk reduction, and offers practical, sustainable, and compelling advice for investors old and young. While people often understand the concept of risk in their everyday lives, as investors they often get it completely wrong, focusing on short-term performance or mistaking short-term price fluctuations for long-term risk. Andy Martin's practical advice and entertaining anecdotes make for a good read, one that can be beneficial to both investors and financial advisors.

Jack Tierney
Executive Director, Invesco Unit Trusts

Discard the time-worn admonition that the only path to higher returns is through higher risk. As Andy Martin admirably explains, successful investing—achieving one's financial goals—requires lowering one's risk. And, unlike many human endeavors, you can get better at investing, even as you age. You don't have to agree with everything Andy says, but you will be well-served if you follow his recommendations about key topics such as diversification, why you must divorce your emotions from your investment decisions, and the value of a good financial advisor.

Robert Huebscher
CEO, Advisor Perspectives;
former president and CEO, Thomson Financial

What is investment risk and why do we automatically assume that it always leads to reward? This book answers those crucial questions. It also effortlessly assassinates populist conventional wisdom. Open any page of this book and you will be simultaneously educated and enlightened. Both individual investors and financial professionals will greatly benefit from Andy's wisdom.

Ron DeLegge II
Founder and Chief Portfolio Strategist, ETFguide.com

Andy Martin has a gifted way with words and advice when it comes to the fundamentals of investments and investment strategies. Dollarlogic is a book that investors of all ages and sophistication levels can benefit from.

Susan Woltman Tietjen
Chairman & Chief Executive Officer, Girard Securities, Inc.

Andy Martin's book is highly enjoyable and readable for the individual investor and investment professional. He provides a unique perspective of profitable investing that we can all learn from.

Victor Ricciardi
co-editor of the book *Investor Behavior: The Psychology of Financial Planning and Investing*

Andy Martin presents some very useful investing advice, such as the shocker that risk—however measured—does not buy you higher returns. Like Odysseus tying himself to a mast to avoid the tempting Sirens, we benefit from anticipating our biases doing simple things like outsourcing our investment tactics. Most people who are good at making money are inefficient investors, and would be better served by the few principles covered in this book.

Eric Falkenstein,
PhD, Portfolio Manager and author of
The Missing Risk Premium

DOLLARLOGIC

~

A Six-Day Plan to Achieving

Higher Investment Returns

by Conquering Risk

~

By

ANDY MARTIN

CAREER PRESS

DOLLARLOGIC

EDITED BY JODI BRANDON

TYPESET BY EILEEN MUNSON

Cover design by Howard Grossman
Printed in the U.S.A.

To order this title, please call toll-free 1-800-CAREER-1 (NJ and Canada: 201-848-0310) to order using VISA or MasterCard, or for further information on books from Career Press.

The Career Press, Inc.
12 Parish Drive
Wayne, NJ 07470
www.careerpress.com

Library of Congress Cataloging-in-Publication Data

CIP Data Available Upon Request.

CONTENTS

THINK

PLAN

Execute

*D*ollarlogic in One Page

*D*ollarlogic in One Page

You have heard it your entire life, and it is wrong. Risk does *not* equal reward. If it did, why would you wear a seat belt?

What is risk? Risk is not only the *worst* that can happen, but what is *most likely* to happen. If negative results equal higher risk, positive results equal lower risk.

Because stocks are likelier to earn higher long-term returns than bonds (4% yearly average for 40-year rolling periods) stocks are *less* risky than bonds.

Short term, however, stocks are unpredictable; math is against you. A loss of 10% has more impact than a gain of 10%, so the key is to reduce losses, not to increase returns.

Does that mean that as a stock investor you now have to predict the markets? No. No one can do that, not even the experts. You only have to predict yourself, such as when do you want to retire, what are your objectives, and how much income do you need? Success or failure, therefore, is dependent on you, not your investments.

So, what should you do? Do as the ultra-wealthy do: Hire an advisor to help you predict *you* and your future, and diversify properly. Do-it-yourselfers have only a map; those with advisors have a GPS—they know where they are *on* the map.

Result? Your future is not dependent on chance or luck because you have systematically reduced risk with diversification and dedicated professional help. Managing risk in this new, more productive way is what I call *dollarlogic.*

Risk equals reward. Well, maybe not. Andy Martin makes compelling arguments here that could change your mind.

The good news is that if you agree, you may be on your way to less volatility, less disruption from your monthly routine of opening your brokerage statements, but more restful sleep. However, his lower-your-risk strategy is not a call to surrender but a call to measure risk by probable outcomes instead of by infrequent negative events, which is how risk is usually defined. Therefore, if you increase your chances of reaching your investment goals, you are reducing your risk—even if this means owning more stocks. I'll bet you have never thought of risk this way.

Andy quotes approvingly Shelby Davis, who said, "You make most of your money in a bear market; you just don't realize it at the time." Warren Buffett might have said the same. I would agree with both. It is not just that you buy low; it is also that you do not sell low. Why not? Because the stock market is nothing to fear. You don't move out of your house if real estate values fall. Andy imagines your investment portfolio as your virtual home that provides warmth, protection, security, and stability. Perhaps you should think of this the next time you are ready to jettison a blue chip stock or well-managed fund the next time it drops in value. Those drops in value are often temporary. You make them permanent when you sell.

Andy has a contrary way of thinking. I have a contrary way of thinking. Most of my professional life I have been pleasantly surprised to discover that thinking differently and acting differently yields positive results, as long as you have the data to back it up. For example *The Laffer Curve* is contrary to conventional thinking. No one would guess that lowering taxes actually increases tax revenues. However, the data back up this claim and provide a reminder to think differently.

One way to make negatives smaller and to achieve potentially higher returns over time is by diversifying. You may not be surprised to learn that widely diversifying your portfolio into stocks, bonds, cash, real estate, and commodities could lower your volatility. However, you will be surprised to see that in the past 45 years this well-diversified portfolio that Andy describes had a higher value than the S&P 500 roughly 70% of the time. In other words, it lowered risk and increased return.

Additionally, you may be surprised to know that as we sit at base camp at what may be a long upward interest rate climb that Andy's research indicates that for long-term investors rising rates are not to be feared either. Again, he shows that broad diversification is a timeless remedy for rising rates.

We said, in our prologue to our book, *An Inquiry Into the Nature and Causes of the Wealth of States: How Taxes, Energy, and Worker Freedom Change Everything* (John Wiley & Sons, Inc., 2014), "To us, a small truth is preferable to a great falsehood, and yet others would seem to prefer complex error to simple truth." I see herein many small truths.

Over my long career I have uncovered perils and opportunities worldwide around every corner of the financial markets. Similarly, Andy Martin's observations will read as travelogue of a memorable and fruitful journey.

Arthur B. Laffer, PhD

This is not a book.

This is a six-day investment management plan. First, I will attempt to change the way you *think.* Then I will help you create a new *plan.* Finally you will begin to *execute* your plan. If all goes well your life will turn out better than had you not read *Dollarlogic.* That would make me immeasurably happy.

However, we need to do this in order. We need to create a firm philosophical foundation about investing, then build upward. But, again, great news: You are done in six days. My recommendation is that you read one chapter a day. You may rest on the seventh!

Let's get started.

Which would you rather have: $2,794,204 or $116,120? That's what $10,000 would have grown to in the stock market or returned in savings accounts respectively—a 24-fold difference in 50 years, roughly your investing lifetime.[1] Despite this, there is almost $3 trillion in low-yielding savings accounts[2]; 52 percent of American households have saved $25,000 or less for retirement[3]; 31 percent have zero or negative financial wealth[4]; and 40 percent of households with annual incomes of $35,000 or less believe that winning a lottery or sweepstakes is the "best chance to obtain a half-million dollars or more."[5]

Social Security, our nation's retirement plan, is in trouble, too. Though stocks have consistently outperformed bonds since 1935 when Social Security was introduced, a U.S. Congressman actually said the "stock market is a risky business.... Social Security benefits must not be jeopardized by stock market ups and downs."[6] He said this despite the fact that stocks have grown *100 times* more than Treasury bills since 1935.

How could there be so much confusion about investing and wealth accumulation?

From 1982 to 2007 (my first 25 years in the investment business), the U.S. stock market achieved what *U.S. News & World Reports* called "America's Bull Run... a financial and economic boom that was as powerful as it was unexpected. During that generational span, the economy more than doubled in size—rising from $5.2 trillion to $11.7 trillion, adjusted for inflation—as the stock market generated an incredible 2,300 percent total return."[7] Was that the best 25 years in the stock market? Not by a long shot.

After 25-plus years the best ideas I've learned about investing have come not from research firms, or specialized training, but from watching my wealthiest clients manage and grow their estates. This is what sets this book apart: My lessons come straight from successful investors over a career completely devoted to helping clients manage money.

In other words, this is real.

I came from a family of risk takers. My father was a crack stunt flyer and U.S. Air Force tanker pilot. He once landed a KC-97 Stratotanker on an ice patch at Dow Air Force Base in Bangor, Maine, when he was attached to the 308th Air Refueling Squadron of the 2d Bombardment Wing. I had three brothers. The oldest was a Navy aviator who bested my pop by landing A-4 Skyhawks on aircraft carriers. The next brother bested my oldest brother by landing in an alfalfa field in Eloy, Arizona (without deploying his parachute). My youngest brother (a former world record holder in motorcycle drag racing) bested him by spearing his helmet (with his head in it) into the back windshield of a car at 120 miles an hour on a busy street in Nashville, Tennessee. He beat my skydiving brother. He lived.

I was different. I have always been risk averse: no broken bones, no major surgeries, no injuries, no excitement, no stories—nothing. Perhaps this is because I have seen so much risk around me. My dad carries a knife in his pocket. I carry a BandAid in my wallet. Much like Paul Varjak from *Breakfast at Tiffany's,* I have always been the "sensitive, bookish type." The closest that I got to physical risk was looking up the word *risk* in my 11-pound *Compact Oxford English Dictionary* and, in my excitement, almost dropping the book from its spindly Bombay Company

pedestal onto my toe. Thus, I wanted to call this book *Risk &
Other Four-Letter Words,* but former Citicorp CEO Walter
B. Wriston beat me to that title.

This is about risk—managing risk. The word *risk* appears
in this book 355 times. My thesis is simple: If you want to
manage risk long-term you need to invest. And if you learn
that *risk does not equal reward,* your life will be better. You
might even find that money can buy a little happiness. Those
who believe money cannot buy happiness probably have very
little of either.

I started in the investment business in August 1982. The
S&P 500 rose 8.7% in one week just two months later, one of
the best one-week records in the stock market.[1] This was the
same year that Steven Spielberg's *ET: The Extra-Terrestrial*
came out. It is fitting that this other-world stock market that
grew into one of the great bull markets should start the same
year that *ET* came out. As good as it was, in truth the 25-year
period ending December 31, 2007, *America's Bull Run,* was
only slightly better than average, but it makes a nice back
story. (The best 25-year period ended December 31, 1999,
with the S&P 500 gaining 17.25% yearly.)[2]

You might say, then, that I am spoiled and only recognize
the stock market when the little numbers on the computer
stock quote screen are green and have little plusses by them,
but it hasn't all been easy. In exchange for the 13% annual
market returns, my clients suffered through, in 25 years, half
of the biggest one-day falls in the history of the Dow Jones
Industrial Average, the first time in history that the three

major stock markets (Dow Jones Industrial Average, S&P 500, and the Nasdaq) were down three years in a row, two (very expensive) wars, and 9/11. Next, in year 26, were the great mortgage meltdown, the worst one-year return in the S&P 500 since 1931, and the worst 10-year return in the S&P 500 in its history.

It is from watching my clients optimize the good times and survive the bad times that I convey these investment principles. And they are indeed principles that can be easily taught and easily learned.

There are many books about investing. The books tell you how Warren Buffett became the world's authority on value investing, how Peter Lynch developed a sixth sense about the market with Fidelity mutual funds, how John Bogle popularized index funds, and how Donald Trump inherited $10 million and leveraged his way to the top in a rising Manhattan real estate market. If you read their stories all you have to do is put down the book and go do the same thing—that is if your circumstances, resources, and timing exactly match theirs. Or you can mimic Jean Paul Getty. "My formula for success?" he said, "Rise early, work late, strike oil."

There is certainly something to learn from each of those books, but you *cannot* follow their paths as a passive investor and achieve their level of success. Their success is too personal, discrete, and time and context sensitive. Trying to divine and apply their secrets is like trying to tap the power of a racehorse, yet as writer Frederick C. Klein lamented, "The worst part about writing about horseracing is that you can't interview the athletes."

With the principles in this book you can be you instead. You can apply each of the lessons found in this book and achieve greater success than you otherwise would.

My premise is this: Risk does not equal reward. My wealthy clients know it. They taught it to me. It's how they got wealthy. It is how you may either get rich or stay rich. You won't understand this by simply memorizing it and reciting it; you must approach this from multiple angles so it has reference points and will stick.

Keep in mind as you read this that I am not a financial writer; I am an investment advisor. Financial writers say stuff like "Never buy variable annuities"—but they have never paid out a death benefit that was higher than the account value to a grieving widow, nor have they ever delivered tax-deferred returns to their readers. Financial writers say, "Only buy no-load funds," but they don't tell you that no-load also means no help, and that you have not improved your odds of success by buying them, or that even no-load funds have expenses. Financial writers say instead of buying "expensive" whole or universal life insurance to "buy term insurance and invest the difference"—but they don't mention that most people out-live term insurance and that the savings rate is dreadfully low, so the net return from that advice is wasted premiums.

What many financial writers don't understand, because they don't get to test their perfect theories, is that people have two parts: reason and emotion. Financial writers deal with reason (sometimes), but investment advisors have to deal with emotions and the results of investor decisions long after the writer is on to the next assignment about electric cars, women's shoes, or the best low-fat hot dog.

Nor is this a "my algorithms are better than your algorithms book." I do not try to baffle you into submission with startling complexity. I would rather serenade you with simplicity.

This is not an auto-biography or an attempt to make a *Donald* of myself. There are many charts and graphs in this book, but they should be used as a shorthand visual cue, not as an exhaustive proof of a position. I am not interested in being right, nor should you. I am only interested in being effective. When you deal with people I have concluded that successful investing is more about investor behavior than superior investment products.

An astounding 97% of investors admit that they need to be better informed when it comes to investing.[3] If I can help you become better informed, or at least help you ask more effective questions, this will be a valuable experience.

THINK

~

Risk ≠ Reward—Understand Risk:
It Is Not What You Think

> "To him who looks at
> the world rationally
> the world looks
> rationally back."
> —Georg Wilhelm Friedrich
> Hegel

Risk does not equal reward.

The phrase is illogical. Instead, if you wish to unite the words to their meanings, the phrase should read *risk = risk,* or *reward = reward.* Any other association of the words is sophistry or salesmanship. The investment industry, being the chief promoter of this errant formula, should stop using it, because it is misleading and simply wrong.

Philosopher Ludwig Wittgenstein's elegant principle of logic yields this simple truth: A is the same as A. This is sometimes expressed in the symbols of logic: $A \equiv A$ where "$\equiv$" means congruence or two subjects of equal identity. To the contrary, it is absurd to say that risk is congruent with reward, or that risk is identical to reward. Worse, the assertion that risk = reward makes investors believe that dangling at the end of risk is inevitable reward, or that one must necessarily pass through the gauntlet of peril to reach promise on the other side.

Risk = reward associates risk with something positive and links the two as if they were necessary co-ingredients, like water + flour = bread.

I am risk averse. You should be, too. Remember what we are talking about: Your investment is your hard-earned money. If you do not do this right you may never have any more money on which to practice. And, according to a recent AARP survey, "[r]unning out of money (is) worse than death."[1] There is no quicker way to run out of money than to take big risks.

What Is Risk?

It is important to know what risk is and what risk is not. Faulty characterizations of risk lead to undesired results. This is how many stock averse investors think:

> *Risk is volatility.*
>
> *Stocks are volatile.*
>
> *Therefore, stocks are risky.*

Instead, risk must be measured against returns. For example, the notion that Treasury bills are low risk is simply untrue when you factor in the return. In Japan and currently for some bonds in the United States, bond yields are so low that only the principal is returned. So what is risked is any potential of return. One could hardly call this a low-risk *investment*— that is, if your purpose is to increase your wealth.

Since biblical times, investment return assumes some quantity received in addition to the principal—the lesser of that quantity, the worse the investment. Recall the parable of the nobleman and his three servants from the Book of Luke. The first servant returned 10 *mina* (*mina* was the equivalent of roughly three months' wages) more than was given him; the second servant returned five *mina* more; the third servant returned only the original *mina*. The nobleman's severe response to the risk-averse third servant was, "Why then didn't you put my money on deposit, so that when I came back, I could have collected it with interest? Take his *mina* away from him and give it to the one who has 10 *mina*." Think of that story while we discuss the relevant definition of risk for savers and investors.

A New Way of Thinking About Risk

Risk is the possibility of suffering loss or harm. Risk is a *relative*, not an absolute, measure. Dying, for example, is not a risk. Dying is an absolute: We will all die. If someone asks you what your probability of dying is, your answer would be 100%. However, if someone asked you what your probability of dying within 10 years, or in a car accident, or after viewing your 401(k) account balance, this is an entirely different question, and needs a complex calculation. Risk is measured only in relation to events, consequences, or time. The risk of dying escalates with certain factors such as smoking, not wearing seatbelts, eating fatty foods, and so forth. Therefore, it is not the risk of dying that should cause concern; it is the risk of some unwanted event leading to an early death.

Think of it this way: Would you rather be in a car crash or a plane crash? If you answered *car crash,* the next question is: Would you rather travel one million miles by car or by plane? If you answered *by plane,* I might ask why, as you just said that cars are less perilous. You might respond, *It depends. If I am traveling 5 miles to a friend's house I would rather take the car, but if I am going to travel an eight-state region over a 10-year sales career it would be safer to fly.* And you would be right.

The Boeing Company claims that it is 22 times safer to fly than it is to drive on a per-mile basis. Fewer people have died in commercial airplane accidents over the past 60 years than are killed in U.S. auto accidents over a typical three-month period. Another study indicates that you have the same chances of dying in a car (one in a million, a *MicroMort*) having traveled only 240 miles, versus traveling 7,500 miles by commercial aircraft.[2] How can this be? Which one is actually safer? How can it be that sometimes driving is safer and at other times an air travel is safer?

Cars are not safer than airplanes. Airplanes are not safer than cars. Instead, safety (or risk) is dependent on the distance traveled. Again to accurately assess risk you always have to measure against the objective. If the objective is a short trip, driving is safer. If the objective is a long trip, flying is safer.

This is much like the benefits of exercise. Exercise is short-term risky when measured against chance of injury, and long-term healthy when adding back the net health benefits. You have a greater chance of injury if you take a 3-mile run or spend an hour in the gym lifting weights versus staying at home and sitting on the couch. To put a number to it, "More than 3.5 million (sports) injuries each year, which cause some loss of time of participation, are experienced by (children and teens)."[3] However, long-term exercise is a proven contributor to cardiovascular health, weight control, muscle and bone strength, lower blood pressure and cholesterol, and even relieving depression. Time converts the greater short-term injury risk into a longer-term health benefit. Can you see how risk is actually lower long term by taking part in short-term "risky" exercising?

Risk, then, because it is a relative term, should be measured as a function of the objective. In this case the relative measure is time. As an investor, how much time will it take for you to grow your principal? What will happen over the long term? In 10, 20, 30 years from now, what will your needs be for your money? The objective is not, not (sorry for the double negative) to lose money on any given day. The objective is to reach your long-term goals. Therefore the safest and most reliable way to do that should be preferred.

Never Bring a Knife to a Gun Fight

There are multiple ways to visualize this new definition of risk. Is a gun or a letter opener riskier? It depends. If you replied *gun,* which would you rather have if someone attacked you? Most would agree that a gun is a more reliable way to neutralize a dangerous threat than a letter opener. Which is riskier: a vitamin or tetracycline? Would you rather your baby swallow a vitamin or tetracycline accidentally? It depends. If she was suffering from an infection you would rather her swallow tetracycline.

Another example: How would you like to have surgery today? Most see surgery as a risky procedure. For starters, you have at least a one in 200,000 chance that you will die if you have surgery.[4] According to the Centers for Disease Control and Prevention, approximately 2 million people a year contract infections during a hospital stay, and more than 90,000 die as the result.[5]

The point is this: You do not decide to have surgery instead of doing nothing; you decide to have surgery instead of suffering the consequences of not having the surgery. Therefore risk is not an event measure (*Do I have surgery or not?*); risk is an outcomes measure (*How will my long-term health be affected?*).

This is the same with investing. You don't invest in the stock market because it is safer. You invest in the stock market because if you do not, you have less likelihood of reaching your financial goals.

Risk: The Noun

Risk is a misunderstood word. How we understand words—more importantly, how we use words—is crucial. If you doubt this, see how the word *love* is used. It is a word so charged with expectation that the mere mention of it can change a relationship. It is the same with the word *risk*. Use both carefully.

How you think about and use the word *risk* will determine what kind of an investor you are. Risk can be a noun, verb, or adjective. My advice is this: Use the word *risk* as a noun and you will have a better future. And, make *you,* not the investment, the subject. When you use the word *risk* regarding investing, ask *Am I putting myself at risk?* Do not ask about a proposed investment *Is this risky?* Don't ask *Are emerging market funds risky?* Ask *Will this emerging market fund put my objectives at risk?* There is a crucial difference.

This will help you focus on you and your investment goals and not on the much-less-critical discussion about the investment vehicle. Plus, you are much more capable of evaluating your own risk tolerance than you are the risk of an investment. Far too much time is spent in comparison of this and that data point of a particular investment. We ask questions such as: What's the beta? What's the 10-year track record? What asset class is it? Better questions are: What income do I need to have in 20 years? What is my current debt level and how can I reduce it? What investment amounts and returns do I need to reach my goals? My recommendation is that you quit asking questions about investments and start asking questions about you. The wealthiest people I know have no more investment knowledge than you do, but they have detailed personal goals, objectives, and plans. They simply match investments to their plan.

A more ideal use of the word *risk* will make the discussion less subjective. You are the object, and your goals, not your investments, are the objective. You are the focus, not your tools. We will see in a later chapter that it is investors who make money, not investments, so begin now to wean yourself off the obsession over the investment rather than you.

I have dealt with clients over the years who tell me, "Andy, I just don't want to take a chance. That's why I am just going to leave everything in CDs. At least then I am not buying something risky." Instead, they should ask, "I wonder if there is anything that I am doing to put my retirement goals at risk. Is investing everything in CDs putting me at risk?"

The answer is Yes. The relative low returns of CDs (certificates of deposit) could put your retirement income at risk. CDs are not risky, but depending on CDs for your future income needs is risky.

Similarly, there is no doubt that driving 10 miles per hour is *less risky* than driving 60 miles per hour. However, you would be putting yourself *at risk* if you drove 10 miles per hour on the interstate. You would also be putting your sick child *at risk* if in an emergency you drove him to the hospital at only 10 miles per hour.

Risk as a condition or state has to be dealt with in much more analytical terms than risk as a discrete act. In other words, doing less-risky things can put you more at risk. The risk of the speed you travel, and the investment you choose, is dependent on the objectives of your journey, and the objectives of your savings goals, respectively.

Stocks are riskier if you need the money for a down payment for a new house at the end of the month and less risky if you need to accumulate more assets over a long period of time. The right investment (or speed) will become very clear after you have determined your objectives.

Volatility ≠ Higher Returns

Associated with the errant concept that risk equals reward is the related assumption that volatility equals higher reward. Think about this in the physical world. To say that the average must be higher because of greater volatility is irrational. An analogy is average temperatures. Did you know that San Diego has an average temperature of 70.5 degrees and Atlanta has a lower average temperature of 61.3 degrees? (See Figure 1-1.) Therefore, temperatures in San Diego are more volatile, right? This must be the case if higher volatility equals a higher average, right? Wrong.

The Atlanta Chamber of Commerce is famous (or notorious) for selling the International Olympic Committee (IOC) on this hilarious notion. Atlanta convinced the IOC before the 1996 Summer Olympics that the temperatures were much cooler than they are by averaging in nighttime temperatures. Athletes would soon discover that 65-degree nights don't make up for 100-degree days.

Greater Volatility ≠ Higher Average

Average	Atlanta	San Diego
Monthly Low / High Temperature	33.5° / 89.4°	48.9° / 77.5°
Annual Temperature	61.3°	70.5°

Figure 1-1

The greater volatility in Atlanta's weather should mean *higher* average temperatures if it is settled science that greater volatility = greater returns. Atlanta average daytime temperatures are much more extreme than San Diego temperatures, but Atlanta is cooler on average.

What I am suggesting by analogy is that there is a San Diego way to invest. You can get to a comfortable room temperature from consistent 68-degree days more reliably than you can get to 68 degrees from an uncomfortable combination of 33-degree and 90-degree days. There is another way to reap higher returns than through unpredictability and numerical frontal assaults on your life savings.

Risk Is a Function of Time

Risk needs to be measured against not just loss, but the timing of loss. For example, life insurance policies don't protect the insured from dying. Nor do the policies assume that the person will live forever. Life insurance policies protect against an *early* death.

However, the risk measure for the timing of life insurance policies is opposite of the timing for stock investments. Visualizing this helps to understand the time connection of risk for stock investing. Nothing beats the returns from premiums paid into life insurance policies that pay off early. And nothing beats the returns from stocks that pay off late. The odds are in your favor the longer you invest. Thus, the risk of life insurance increases over time, but decreases over time with stocks.

How is this incremental value for stocks valued over time? Using history as our guide (and it is the best guide we have) there was a 3:1 chance that the stock market rose in any given year, and a 100% chance that you would have made money for any 20-year period or more.

Why is this important? Because of this: The average 65-year-old couple can expect to live another 19 years. In addition, there is a 50:50 chance that one member of the couple will live beyond 92, and a 25% chance that he or she will live beyond 97.[6] You need stocks now more than ever because you are going to live longer. No generation until now has ever had to anticipate living in retirement for 30 years, but Social Security now only replaces about 40% of pre-retirement income for today's average worker.

For a wider perspective, over the last 85 years stocks were up 72% of the time, down 28% of the time, beat 5% returns 68% of the time, and had an arithmetic average yearly return of 11.50%.[7] Getting theses odds in your favor will lower your risk.

Real-World Risk

My belief is risk does not equal reward, and I am attempting to change the way you think about risk. But, let's get back to the real world for a minute before I get into too much investment detail. Let me ask you if risk = reward with a few questions:

- Do you ride motorcycles without a helmet?

- Are you happy when your daughter introduces you to her new tattooed, out-of-work, ex-felon boyfriend?

- Do you juggle chainsaws as a hobby?

- Do you drink alcohol by the bottle rather than by the glass?

- Do you refuse to wear eye protection when you use your weed-eater around the yard?

- Do you walk close to the edge of cliffs when you hike?

- Do you avoid sunscreen on a long day at the beach?

- Do you fix shingles on your roof on the day of a snowstorm?

- Do you leave your doors unlocked and outside lights off every night?

- Do you exaggerate and lie on job applications?

- Do you eat junk food at every meal?

- Do you refuse to wear seatbelts?

Your answer, I am guessing, was *no* for all or most of these questions. Each question was the same: *Are you a risk taker?* Notice that there is virtually no part of your life in which you seek risks. Instead, you avoid risks as a good habit. So, how could it be that in one very narrow but vital part of your life it would pay to ignore everything you believe? How could it be that investing is that one area of your life where taking big risks is advised?

Risk and Business

Even though you might agree that risk taking should not be a part of your daily routine, you might still believe that the world of business is different. Hollywood portrays businesspeople as tycoons, wildcatters, roughnecks, devil-may-care opportunists who, from taking huge risks, reap astounding, lavish rewards. Advertising genius Don Draper, from the television hit *Mad Men,* stuns prospective clients with a provocative pitch off the top of his head. One crazy risqué appeal and—bingo—he closes a huge new advertising deal with General Motors. He shoots from the hip, is dead-eye accurate, and is a winner.

That's not how it works. As the son of a successful businessman, I saw how it really works my entire life. I watched my father systematically, methodically, intentionally, and purposefully wring as much risk out of his business that he could with strict inventory control instead of foolhardy buying; add staff only when absolutely necessary; be an early adopter of free marketing and sales (the internet); reinvest profits; offer exclusive products that would allow higher margins; and always seek the niche that was underserved rather than the most popular, which was highly competitive *and* risky. The results were rewards for his entire working and retired life. I learned from my father that low risk = high reward.

You don't know my father, but maybe you know of Ted Turner—the founder of WTBS and CNN, and one of the largest land owners in the United States. Writer Malcolm Gladwell illustrates the test case in business risk avoidance in a *New*

Yorker article called "The Sure Thing: How Entrepreneurs Really Succeed." Turner is the model of risk management and avoidance—the real Ted Turner, not the mythic Ted Turner you know—the big sky, big dreaming, "mouth of the south" risk-on rancher. When you discover how Turner saved his father's billboard business, with no money, from a predator who tried to take advantage of his father's suicide when Turner was only 24; financed his first television station (WJRJ, Channel 17, in Atlanta) with no cash; and purchased the Atlanta Braves baseball team with a down payment from the Braves, not from Turner, you start to see how his empire was built on the risks and money of others, not him.

How? As Gladwell says, "It's because Turner is a cold-blooded bargainer who could find a million dollars in someone's back pocket that the person didn't know he had. Once you get past the more flamboyant aspects of Turner's personal and sporting life, in fact, there is little evidence that he had any real appetite for risk at all."[8] Gladwell explains, "Successful entrepreneurs are seen as bold gamblers; in reality, they're highly risk-averse.... Would we so revere risk-taking if we realized that the people who are supposedly taking bold risks in the cause of entrepreneurship are actually doing no such thing?"[9]

The Investment Industry's Perception of Risk

Sometimes the investment industry seems confused about risk. In some ways the investment industry's perception of risk is like the tobacco industry. It would make sense because the industries are equally over-regulated by the federal government. Therefore, we are left with a confusing mix of schizophrenic feelings whenever we see an advertisement. For example, there is a cigarette advertisement that shows two coquettishly placed pink and turquoise cigarette packs surrounded by playful dancing roses with the description "light & luscious." This ad is presumably targeting girls. How do we know? Beneath the ad's eerie likeness to Joe Camel meets Barbie's Malibu Beach House is the ominous Surgeon General's warning that reads *"Smoking by Pregnant Women May Result in Fetal Injury, Premature Birth, and Low Birth Weight."*

The *it is really good but it will kill you* approach is so contradictory that consumers block it out. They have a blank reaction to the warning and rationalize *if it were that bad it wouldn't be legal,* and they smoke away. Nor is the industry protected because of this warning. Besides the $200 billion settlement that the industry agreed to in 1998, tobacco companies are still sued daily for millions of dollars despite the fact that they have been telling their customers that their product will kill you for almost 50 years. There are simply no connections among the advertising message, the use of the product, and the forced warning label.

Imagine, likewise, if an airline described flying with the same risk = reward strategy that the investment and tobacco industry uses. Imagine if this was the disclaimer that airlines included with your ticket:

Warning: You are likelier to die or sustain serious injury in an in-flight decompression, explosion, fuselage break, or accident than from a similar automobile crash. There is no assurance that your travel objectives can be met with this airline. Consult with a travel agent before purchasing a ticket.

No one would support this kind of disclaimer. Even consumer safety groups that are overly cautious have not lobbied for this kind of disclosure. Why? I think it is because the airline industry believes in itself more than the investment industry does, and has done a better job of building the safety case for flying. Flying is safer for long trips. Period. The over-preening federal government tends to agree, so no disclaimer necessary. Because the investment industry is so unaware of the true nature of risk, which is not *price volatility*, but is instead *the odds that you will reach your investment goals with any given investment,* we acquiesce to confusing and counterproductive disclosures.

Mutual fund prospectuses are where this is most evident. The prospectus for a popular short-term bond fund is 101 pages long, whereas the prospectus for another popular emerging-markets 3x leveraged bear market fund is 88 pages long—13 pages shorter. Just so you know (because you wouldn't know from the prospectus), the leveraged emerging markets fund is radically more volatile than the bond fund. From December 30, 2008, to December 31, 2012, the leveraged emerging markets fund was *down* 98.48%. In contrast, for the last 10 years the bond fund has grown like an oak tree: slowly and steadily.

I am not saying that the bond fund is more desirable, will perform better, or belongs in your 401(k) plan, instead of the emerging markets fund. The problem is neither does the prospectus. You can bet that the bond fund prospectus is not 13 pages longer than the emerging markets prospectus because it takes that many more pages to alert the investor to the risks of government bonds. What you *can* bet is that comparing the prospectuses will not give you any meaningful insight to the differences between the relative risks and rewards of the two funds. That's where we are as an industry 70-plus years after the Investment Company Act of 1940, which defines and codifies regulated investment companies like mutual funds.

I think you can see that if you want to protect yourself against risk you need information of a different sort. Your security against confusion comes from understanding the true nature of investment risk.

We're Off to See the Wizard (of Omaha)

My favorite investor is Warren Buffett, not because he has made the most money, but because he has made the most sense. He may be the greatest investor in history. In his 2007 letter to shareholders for Berkshire Hathaway he wrote, among other memorable gems, that he was looking for a new chief investment officer to replace him. How did he describe such a replacement? He was looking for a person "genetically programmed to recognize and avoid risks," who shows "independent thinking, emotional stability, and a keen understanding of both human and institutional behavior."[10] This is, in other words, a summary of Warren Buffett's personal investment temperament and expectations, and how he grew to be the world's wealthiest investor. How did he do it? He avoided risk.

One apparent choice was Todd Combs. Todd Combs surprised Wall Street because he only managed $280 million before the Berkshire Hathaway offer. But, the choice did not surprise me because Combs has an able background in insurance, worked for the state of Florida's comptroller, and has experience managing a portfolio of financial companies. In short, he is a risk manager.

Think about that. If you asked the average person how one of the wealthiest people on earth managed to accumulate his fortune, most would say that he did so by taking enormous risks with his money. They would be wrong. Warren Buffett does not purposely take risks with his and his shareholders' money.

As evidence, when Berkshire Hathaway, Buffett's company, is categorized (as in the biological hierarchy of family, genus, species, etc.), the *sector* is financial services, the *industry* is reinsurance, and the *type* is "slow growth" according to Morningstar, Inc. "Slow growth" does not sound like high risk to me, nor would it fall into the risk = reward model. Slow growth is how he does it. Slow growth is how we should do it.

Then Does More Risk = More Reward?

Meet Ralph Shive, a *Barron's Top 100 Manager*, who recently held a top spot in his Morningstar, Inc. category over three-, five-, and 10-year time periods. Shive said he "learned to embrace that idea that risk is losing money."[11] This does not mean that he is a conservative investor. To the contrary, Shive is described as "reasonably aggressive, meaning that he's aggressive about making money and also aggressive about preserving it."[12] Note that "high risk" and "aggressive" are not necessarily the same thing. In my experience bigger risks are taken by being too conservative than by being too aggressive. I am not talking about risks from day-to-day price volatility. I am talking about something worse: risks to future income, risks to standard of living, risks to buying power, risks to financial independence, and ultimately risks to your security and legacy. I think Mr. Shive would agree with that.

Do Not Exaggerate Risk or Rewards

CNN just reported that the Dow plunged 45 points. What did they not say? They did not say that the Dow dropped .0028 or .28% or $28 of your $10,000 investment. Why? Which data is more useful: a number like 45 without any comparative reference, or a percentage like .28% that gives scale to an increase or decrease? Certainly percentages are more useful than standalone numbers, but the media is inclined to manufacture a story out of every data point. Forty-five points is a story. Forty-five points seems like a lot. If a basketball team won by 45 points it would be extraordinary; .28% however is statistically insignificant—which is exactly my argument. If the media changed overnight to reporting the stock market in percentages instead of raw numbers, eventually they would just stop reporting. Who cares if the market is up or down .28%?

As long as the media talks in terms of the Dow *plunging* or *soaring,* then they exaggerate risk and reward. This is not helpful. Why? *Plunge* talk worries those who are already nervous, and *soar* talk puffs up those who imagine that they are in a parade every time they see a ticker tape. Who would ever fly in an airplane if it was described in these terms: *Fly now if you want to plunge to the ground or soar through the clouds?* Besides the transparent desires of the media, if either risks or rewards are either intentionally mischaracterized or simply unknown, then conclusions are naturally erroneous.

Another problem is how we quantify risk and reward. We take risks that are too great for so little reward. Fix that by making a realistic assessment of the reward first, then work backward. We have been so programmed to automatically think that risk = reward that we have also grown to believe that more risk = more reward.

Here is an example. Years ago my oldest brother and I took a trip to San Antonio and the Austin Chalk area of Texas to evaluate investing in an oil well for him. It was a fun and most unprofitable trip. The problem was not just that we did not understand the risk (tip: Don't invest in a single well), we also exaggerated the reward. Oil will do that. Anyone who saw *Giant* or *Dallas* or the *Beverly Hillbillies* can gin up images of a miraculous life makeover courtesy of a lone deep well spring of Texas tea.

This was not the fault of the oil company executive. He showed us *pro formas* that illustrated 10–15% annual returns if it struck oil. I remember the numbers not being far off from what most stock mutual funds were projecting at the time. Honestly I think when we looked at the spreadsheets we weren't seeing rows of numbers; we were seeing Elly May Clampett or Charlene Tilton. When you exaggerate the rewards you will take more risks than you should. Moral: Excitable people should hire someone to make their investment decisions.

Does Figure 1-2 Contradict Me?

Here is another way to think about this. Risk ≠ Reward. Or does it? Figure 1-2 is the type of chart used in the investment industry that tries to convince people to invest in stocks. I am trying to convince you to invest in stocks,

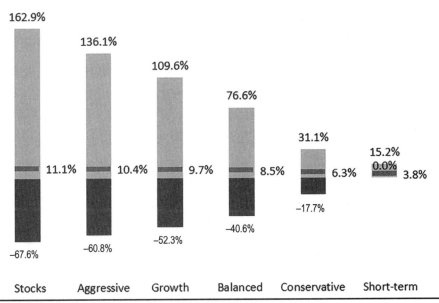

Historical Investment Returns[13]

Bars show high, low, average range of 12-month returns for each asset for period 1926–2001, not necessarily calendar years.

Figure 1-2

too—although, you will see, not *only* stocks in later chapters. However, I do not like charts like these because they only tell you what investments returned, not what investors returned. I have never had an investment for a client, only investors, so I am more concerned with what happens to people than I am with what happens to financial instruments.

Note the relative difference between the highest and lowest return range, and the average annual return range. We have been coaxed into believing (in this case, mostly by my industry) that risk = reward, illustrated here as highest and lowest annual returns equal higher average returns. To me this chart illustrates the opposite. It tells me that the extremes in returns are not worth the marginal returns. The question is not *Should I invest all stocks or all short term (presumably meaning money market funds or bonds)?* The better question is *What mix of investments will most likely help me reach my investment objectives?* The person who buys in to this chart and goes 100% all stocks will be out of the market, maybe forever, if his portfolio ever drops by 67.6% (the worst 12-month return). If he sells after dropping 67.6%, he is much less likely to reach his goal. I do not like the approach that says, in essence, if you can survive a 67-foot fall then you can climb to the top of this 162-foot mountain. It creates false choices.

What really happens when investors' portfolios drop so precipitously is that they give up. Note these revealing charts. These charts measure what happens to investors, not just what happens to investments. Morningstar, Inc. calls this relationship the IR–TR gap for investor return–total return gap. (See Figure 1-3.) IR is how the investor did, and TR is how the investment did. You can see that the Investor Return was higher than the Total Return with low-risk (standard deviation) funds, despite the fact that the higher-risk funds have slightly higher returns. In other words, the *lower* the risk the higher return—to the investor. Don't forget: It is the investor that counts (you), not the investment.

Investor Returns vs. Fund Returns[14]

	Investor Returns	Fund Returns	IR – TR Gap
Low Standard Deviation Funds	5.97%	6.21%	0.24
High Standard Deviation Funds	4.32%	6.28%	1.96

Figure 1-3

In Figure 1-4 shown on page 46, notice the relative returns between U.S. sector funds and balanced funds. Though the higher risk (sector funds) had a higher return, the *lower* risk (balanced funds) had a higher investor return.

Figure 1-5 also shown on page 46 tells a similar story for an entire decade. Note that in only one case (balanced funds) did investor return actually meet or exceed the returns of the investment itself. In every other fund type investors underperformed; they bought and sold at the wrong times.

Investor Returns vs. Fund Returns by Funds Types[15]

Fund Types	Investor Returns	Fund Returns	IR–TR Gap
U.S. Diversified	6.03	7.3	−1.27
U.S.Sector	6.75	9.53	−2.78
Balanced	**7.88**	**7.8**	**0.08**
Intl. Diversified	10.83	11.29	−0.46
Intl. Regional	10.6	11.38	−0.78
Taxable Bond	5.13	5.47	−0.34
Municipal Bond	4.29	4.45	−0.16
All Funds	6.59	7.49	−0.9

Figure 1-4

Investor Returns vs. Fund Returns[16]

Category	Investor	Fund Return
U.S. Equity Funds	0.22	1.59
Intl. Equity Funds	2.64	3.15
Balanced	**3.36**	**2.74**
Alternative	8.07	8.55
Taxable Bond	4.00	5.33
Municipal	2.96	4.57
All Funds	1.68	3.18

Figure 1-5

The point is that investors (again, we are talking about *you* now) don't stick around with investments that are volatile, high risk, or otherwise scary. Because you are an investor, not an investment, focus on what happens to investors, not to investments. We will see how to create a more positive investor experience than the false risk = reward choices that you have been instructed to endure.

Stocks Are Less Risky Than Bonds

Your Objectives, Not the Investment, Determine the Investment's Risk

> "You have to get a little
> inflated or you'll never get
> off the ground."
> —James Hillman

Stocks are less risky than bonds.

I did not get that backward. You are used to hearing that stocks are riskier than bonds; I have assumed that stocks are riskier than bonds for so long that, even though I know it is not true, it is hard for me to think, say, or write that *stocks are less risky than bonds.*

Let's get something straight before you read further: I did not say that investing in a one-year certificate of deposit or a U.S. Treasury bill is riskier than investing in a stock. I am not saying that you have a greater chance of losing money in government-insured certificates of deposit than in the stock market.

I *am* saying that you have a greater chance of losing your long-term buying power with government-insured

CDs, money market funds, and U.S. Treasury bills. I *am* saying that the odds of your having a positive return after inflation are greater if you invest in stocks. I *am* saying that, measured against your objectives, investing in stocks is less risky. These distinctions are vital to your future.

The wealthy investors that I have known through the years realize this—after all, they taught it to me. It is so natural for them that it is intuitive. Wealthy investors do not invest in stocks because they are risk tolerant; they invest in stocks because they are low returns intolerant.

Imagine what a destructive force I would have been as an investment advisor if over my entire career I had cajoled every client into buying only money market funds, CDs, and bonds because I believed those investments were less risky and therefore suitable for 100% of my clients' savings. My clients would be impoverished and I would be out of a job. Or, perhaps I could manage the Social Security trust fund.

I think it is a perfectly reasonable conclusion that stocks are less risky than bonds because the returns divided by the time invested are higher. How can an investment with a higher return be riskier than an investment that has a lower return? Stocks are less risky than bonds not just because there is a bigger positive number to the right of the equal sign, but because stocks will more reliably help you reach your objective. I should say, hypothetically, that even if stocks gave a lower rate of return, but better enabled you to reach your objective, then stocks would be still less risky than bonds. The key here is reaching your goals, and how best to do that.

Stocks are less risky than bonds in the same way that air travel is safer than cars, as I mentioned in the last chapter. That is, stocks are not by nature safer than bonds any more than jets are safer than cars. I'd rather crash in a car than in an airplane, but I'd rather travel a million miles by commercial airliner than a car, and it would statistically be safer if I was flying. So, if the question is *Which mode of travel is safer in the long run?*, commercial airlines wins—just as stocks are safer and are *less* risky when you're discussing long-term returns.

You must consider how much risk, or how much *time*, you would have to take to get the same return if you did not invest in stocks. It is true that in the short term stocks are more unpredictable, but as an investor you have to think of risk in terms of time—that is, how long will it take to reach a certain account value? The longer it takes, the riskier it is.

For example, using the "rule of 72" (72% return of the investment = years it will take to double your money) if you received an 8% return on stocks it would take nine years to double your money. However, if you receive a .23% return, which is the yield currently of a one-year U.S. Treasury bill, it will take 313 years to double your money. You decide which investment poses a greater risk to your retirement.

Likewise, to determine risk with investing you must always measure against the objective. If the objective is an assured return of principal in a short period, then a certificate of deposit is safer. If the objective is generating greater retirement assets in the future, then stocks are safer. Yes, *safer.*

I am *not* saying that stocks are riskier than bonds, but if you invest, the rewards will outweigh the risks. That's what the investment industry says. Instead, I am saying that you have a greater chance of reaching your objective of generating greater long-term assets if you invest in equity investments like stocks. By this definition, when you have a greater chance of achieving your objectives, you are taking the *least*-risky, safer path.

Granted, on any given day your investment in a stock is more at risk than your investment in a savings account. That's just like saying you'd rather crash in a car than in an airplane—the car in this case is a bond, and the airplane is the stock. However, if your objective is to generate a superior retirement income, leaving money in a savings account is riskier than investing in the stock market.

Another example is casinos. Although investing in the stock market is often compared to gambling, it is actually the opposite, because the longer you sit at the blackjack table, the worse your odds are, whereas the longer you are invested in stocks, the better your odds.

By the Numbers

It is not even close. In an almost-50-year period an investment in stocks returned 24 times that of savings accounts. A $10,000 investment in stocks would have grown to $2,794,204. The same $10,000 investment would have grown to $116,120 in savings accounts.[1]

- In the 87-year period ending December 31, 2014, stocks returned 147 times Treasury bills. A $100 investment in stocks would have returned $289,995 versus $1,973 for Treasury bills.[2]

- In the last 87 years, the S&P 500 Index has delivered negative returns only four times for a 10-year rolling period. Ninety-five percent of the time for 10-year periods stocks have delivered positive returns.[3]

- Even in bad times stocks have outperformed bonds. Overall since 1928 for every 10-year rolling period (78 periods) stocks have outperformed bonds 83% of the time.[4]

- The best, median, and worst 10-year rolling periods for stocks was better than the best, median, and worst 10-year rolling periods for Treasury bills from 1934 through 2014. Even the worst case for stocks was better than the worst case for Treasury bills.[5]

- Remember this expression: 4, 4, 40. In 40-year rolling periods, stocks outperformed on average (median period) certificates of deposit by fourfold, roughly a 4% average annual return difference.[6]

- For every-40 year period (roughly an investor's contributing life) from December 31, 1927, through December 31, 2014, stocks have been up on average 10.78% with a low of 8.45% and high of 12.46%.[7]

You may have already conceded the long-term advantage to investing in stocks, but you may be surprised to know that even in the short-term stocks are usually advantageous:

- For the last 87 years in each one-year period stocks outperformed Treasury bills 58/87 years, or 67% of the time.[8]

- In the last 87 one-year periods, stocks were up 72% of the time.[9]

- In the last 87 one-year periods stocks have outperformed a 4% return 68% of the time.[10]

Note that all of the stock advantages continued into 2015.

Despite this data, the numbers do *not* speak for themselves. Investing is not a math problem. Investing is a risk-management problem.

If the numbers spoke for themselves I would not have to repeat them here. Everyone would simply review the numbers, invest in stocks, never sell in a bear market, earn higher rates of return rather than inflation, and live happily ever after.

Why don't they? Why do less than half of U.S. households invest in stocks?[11] I believe that the chief reason is that most investors do not understand risk, which is what I am trying to fix in this book.

What About the Great Depression?

I know what you are thinking: *No matter what you say, stocks are more risky than bonds. You investment guys always seem to leave out the Great Depression, when everyone lost money.*

Let's discuss this. What about the 25-year span where stocks did absolutely nothing—the worst 25-year period in market history?[12] From 1929 to 1954 stock prices, though volatile, went nowhere. Talk about a lost generation. What if you get stuck there and it ruins you?

What I am about to say will surprise you. The Dow Jones Industrial Average (DJIA) first traded on May 26, 1896, and closed at 40.94. The all-time low was on August 8, 1896, when it closed at 28.48. On September 3, 1929, the DJIA hit a record peak of 381.17—then went straight down and lost 90% of its value over the next three years. Twenty-five *years* later, on November 23, 1954, the DJIA finally closed again above 381.17 at 382.74. For 25 years the stock market did nothing. And do you know what?

Stocks still beat bonds.

Stock returns have two components: dividends and price movement (or capital appreciation). If a stock is worth $20.00 per share and pays a $1.00-per-share dividend, it yields 5%. Or, if a stock is worth $20.00 per share and goes up by $1.00 per share to $21.00, its value has increased (by capital appreciation) by 5%. Either way, the stock has returned 5% to the investor before tax. We can quibble about which is preferable, more reliable, or more tax efficient—dividends or capital gains—but you can see that either way the return has been 5%.

During the 25-year doldrums (1929–1954) when the stock market added no capital gains through price appreciation (the DJIA went from roughly 381 and back to 381), we need to

Dividend Yields vs. Corp. Bond Yields 1929–1954[13]

	DJIA	AAA Corp. Bond Yield	Stocks Premium
1929	4.10%	4.80%	=0.70%
1930	4.70%	4.50%	0.20%
1931	6.10%	4.60%	1.50%
1932	7.20%	5.00%	2.20%
1933	4.10%	4.50%	=0.40%
1934	3.70%	4.00%	=0.30%
1935	3.80%	3.60%	0.20%
1936	4.30%	3.30%	1.00%
1937	5.30%	3.20%	2.10%
1938	3.80%	3.20%	0.60%
1939	4.30%	3.00%	1.30%
1940	5.20%	2.80%	2.40%
1941	6.20%	2.80%	3.40%
1942	6.00%	2.80%	3.20%
1943	4.70%	2.70%	2.00%
1944	4.60%	2.70%	1.90%
1945	3.90%	2.60%	1.30%
1946	3.90%	2.50%	1.40%
1947	5.20%	2.60%	2.60%
1948	6.40%	2.80%	3.60%
1949	7.10%	2.70%	4.40%
1950	7.50%	2.60%	4.90%
1951	6.30%	2.90%	3.40%
1952	5.70%	3.00%	2.70%
1953	5.80%	3.20%	2.60%
1954	5.20%	2.90%	2.30%
Average	5.20%	3.30%	57% > bonds

Figure 2-1

look at the other component of stock returns: the dividends. As it happens, even though stock prices did not increase, the average dividend yield for stocks was 5.2% during this period. In comparison the average yield on bonds was only 3.3%. (See Figure 2-1. on page 56.)

The result is that even over this 25-year, two-month, and 20-day period where stock prices did not go up, the annual return with dividends reinvested was roughly 6.1%. A $10,000 investment would have grown to $44,480. Stock dividend yields averaged around 5% during this time, but three-month Treasury bills averaged less than 2%, and long-term Treasury bonds averaged less than 4% during this period.[14] Stocks beat bonds even in the worst 25 years in our nation's history. Further, there has never been a 25-year period when Treasury bills have outperformed stocks.

Another Way Stocks Are Less Risky Than Bonds

Investment returns should always be netted against inflation because the wealth-destroying effect of inflation is one of the primary reasons why we have to invest at all. Why? If goods and services didn't cost more in the future, we wouldn't need more money to buy them. The mistake that most people make by not subtracting inflation from their returns is why savings accounts enjoy a better following than they should. There is almost $3 trillion in savings currently. For the decade ending December 31, 2014, for example, savings accounts underperformed inflation, which effectively turned *savers* into *losers*.[15]

If you do not believe that inflation is an important factor, just imagine paying a 3% account management fee every year, or instead of your certificate deposit yielding 4%, it actually yields 1%. Take note: You *are* paying those fees now, in effect, and your CD does not yield 4% after inflation.

Here is a succinct way to illustrate the effect of a 3% inflation rate (the historical average) on a dollar: Remember that dollar bill in your wallet from 1980? It is now worth 40 cents. (See Figure 2-2.)

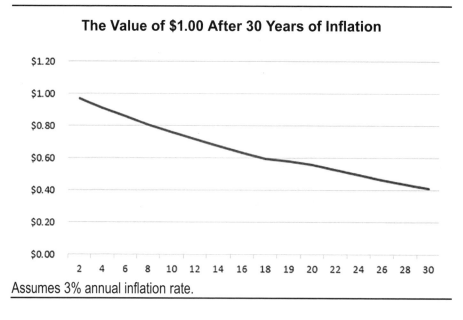

Figure 2-2

The return of an investment, after inflation, is called its *real* return. Stocks are much less risky than bonds in every meaningful period when comparing real returns. We do not have to look over 30 years to prove this.

Many would agree that stocks are a superior investment long term, but they believe that the tradeoff is significant short-term risk. They condition themselves to believe that as long as they can suffer through year after year of losses one day the sun will rise, the clouds will clear, the rain will stop, and they will be better off than if they had not braved the storm. This is not the case.

The reality is this: *There is no greater chance that you will have a negative real rate of return in any given year with stocks than with bonds.* (See Figure 2-3.)

How Stocks, T-Bills, and T-Bonds Perform Against Inflation[16]

	Stocks > Inflation	T-Bills > Inflation	T-Bonds > Inflation
Years out of...	59	51	51
Total years	87	87	87
%	68%	59%	59%

Figure 2-3

Feel free to read that line again if you were daydreaming: *There is no greater chance that you will have a negative real rate of return in any given year with stocks than with bonds.*

You may respond, *Okay, I see that, but the average loss in the down years was greater for stocks than for bonds.* This is true. It is also true that stocks were disproportionately higher in up years. The average positive returns were greater, so much so that once again I must reiterate that over an almost 80-year period that included the Great Depression, deflation, almost 20 recessions, wildly swinging interest rates, multiple wars, stagflation, the Great Recession, and credit crisis, stocks outperformed Treasury bills by an average of 7.24% per year.[17]

Does this surprise you? It shouldn't. Think of it this way: You know that stocks have outperformed bonds over the long run. So how could it be that year after year you add up columns of negative numbers only to get a positive number in the end? In other words, the building blocks of positive returns long term are positive returns short term.

Another interesting wonder in these numbers is that negative real (after inflation) returns for stocks goes down, and eventually vanishes to 0 for 20-year rolling returns. In other words, for the 68 20-year periods from 1928 to 2014 (1928 to 1947, 1929 to 1948, etc.) stocks had a positive real return 100% of the time, whereas 10-Year Treasury bonds had positive real returns 59% of the time and Treasury bills had positive returns 71% of the time for the same rolling 20-year periods.

Therefore, frankly it is very hard to build the case for short-term or long-term investing in 100% fixed income after inflation. In the short or long term, it is difficult to build the case for investing all your savings in low yielding and under-performing assets. In each time period, from one year to rolling 20-year periods, stocks had a greater chance of positive real returns.

Which One Is Riskier, Again?

You don't subtract up your returns; you *add* up your returns. If you are stuck in a money market fund you will never have much to add up. Worse, you are a saver, not an investor. Hint: There are no savers on the *Forbes 400* list, only investors.

Likewise, is it riskier to make investments that occasionally drop in value, or is it riskier to make investments that rarely go up? What's riskier: a bond fund or stock fund? If you have been pre-programmed to answer (before reading this book) that stocks are riskier than bonds, your reflexes will say, *Stock funds are riskier.* What are the real numbers? The average large blend stock fund returned 4.77% yearly; the average ultra-short bond fund returned just 2.48% yearly for the 15 years ending December 31, 2014. Additionally, of the 217 large blend stock funds, only 28 underperformed the average ultra-short bond fund; 87% of the stock funds outperformed the bond funds. And, the lowest performer of the large blend stock funds was not materially worse than the lowest performer of the ultra-short bond funds. (See Figure 2-4 on page 62.)

How could one conclude that bond funds were less risky than stock funds unless your definition of risk does not include superior average returns? Let me remind you (but not overstate) that this doesn't always happen. Stocks underperform bonds at times. Indeed, every large blend stock fund was down in 2008; the average was down 37.19%. However, if you describe risk as having the chance during any time frame of losing money, I believe this will hold you back as an investor. But because the downtimes are rare, it is simply inaccurate to say that stocks are riskier than bonds.

Stock Funds Outperform Bond Funds[18]

Fund Type	# of Funds With 15-year Record	Average	Best	Worst
Large Blend Stock	217	4.77%	13.98%	−0.33%
Ultra-Short Bond	21	2.48%	3.33%	1.14%

87%, or 189, of the large blend stock funds outperformed the average ultra-short bond funds.

Figure 2-4

Therefore, you can see that in many cases we create a false choice when we say that stocks can go down so they are riskier. If instead you describe risk as the chance that I may achieve my investment goals, then we are thinking more alike because now you are focusing on you and your goals, and not the investment. Clearly you would have had a greater chance of achieving your retirement income goals in the 15-year period ending December 31, 2014, had you invested in a large blend stock fund. Therefore, the large blend stock fund was less risky than the ultra-short bond fund.

What About Money Market Funds?

I think you can begin to see that is it is unwise to say, *I can't afford to risk my money, so I will not invest in stocks.* If you only invest in money market funds, certificates of deposit, savings bonds, or the like, whether you can afford to risk your money or not, you could be risking your money. Money market funds were created in the United States in 1971 by Bruce Bent and Henry Brown. Bent oversaw the creation of the *Reserve Fund* and its unfortunate demise in 2008 because of the bankruptcy of Lehman Brothers and the resulting hysteria from the regulators, prosecutors, and elected officials who forced the Reserve Fund out of business.

Money market funds are indeed risky, but not for that reason. Money market funds can be a risky choice when investors use them as their sole long-term investment vehicle. How many investors own money market funds? In 2013, according to the Investment Company Institute, 56.7 million U.S. households owned mutual funds.[19] Money market funds are included in that number with nearly $3 trillion in investor assets. Money market funds (and their equivalents) have a role in long-term money management, but not as a primary investment. We will see this in the chapter on diversification (Day 6).

Money market funds became readily available in 1975. So how have they done since?

Figure 2-5 shows a comparison of the S&P 500 (stocks) versus money market funds for each of the 29 10-year-rolling periods (1975 to 1984, 1976 to 1985, etc.) since 1975.

The results are conclusive. The median case scenario showed stocks nearly tripling the returns of money market funds. The worst case was a loss of 1.38% investment for stocks—and that was from the worst 10 years ever in the stock market. How could someone conclude that stocks are riskier than money market funds?

10-Year Rolling Returns: Money Markets vs. Stocks[20]

	Best $10,000 =	Median $10,000 =	Worst $10,000 =
Money Markets	9.78% / $25,419	4.84% / $16,044	1.37% / $11,463
Stocks	19.19% / $57,854	13.92% / $36,813	−1.38% / $8,700

Figure 2-5

Actually, I have met few people who invest only in stocks, whereas I have met many who invest only in money market funds, CDs, and savings accounts. I have also met (and I encourage) those who invest in stock *and* bonds. A more realistic comparison would be against a mix of 50/50 stocks and bonds. (See Figure 2-6.)

10-Year Rolling Returns: Money Markets vs. 50/50 Stocks and Bonds[21]

	Best $10,000 =	Median $10,000 =	Worst $10,000 =
Money Markets	9.78% / $25,419	4.84% / $16,044	1.37% / $11,463
50/50 Stocks, Bonds	15.95% / $43,932	12.33% / $31,972	2.66% / $12,998

Figure 2-6

For this 39-year period the 50/50 Stocks/Bonds portfolio outperformed money market funds and never had a negative 10-year run, and even its worst 10 years was better than the worst 10 years for money market funds. That is a significant risk/reward ratio and is a classic example of low risk = high reward. This is our first sample of diversification. The argument for diversification will grow day by day in this book, but this is a good primer.

Remember: Risk is a function of probability. Investment risk is not only measured by the *worst* that can happen, but by what is *most likely* to happen. Think of it this way. If you had an employee who showed up for work every day without fail but accomplished little or no sales, is he less risk to your business than a reasonably reliable, albeit with imperfect attendance, employee who produces three times as much? That has been the difference between money market funds and stocks for the last 38 years. Likewise, I think most would prefer the more productive, yet lesser dependable employee.

Who Owns Stocks?

If you are considering investing in stocks you should know that you will be in very good company, or at least wealthy company. Wealthy people own stocks. Only 4.2% of the bottom 20% in income-owned stocks, whereas 45.3% of the top decile in income-owned stocks in the most recent figures.[22]

Do not automatically think that because the bottom 20% are poor that they own nothing: 37.5% of them are homeowners. Additionally, 19.9% own certificates of deposit or savings accounts, or pooled investment funds, or "other"; 19.7% have retirement accounts or cash value in a life insurance policy, and 81.8% have some other financial assets.[23] They just don't choose stocks. Wealthy people own three times the percentage of certificates of deposits, but 10 times the percentage level of stocks. Therefore, it is not just the amount or percentage ownership that is important to note, but the asset choice itself. Wealthy people are much likelier to value stock ownership than less-wealthy people.

Stock owners are more educated, have higher net worth, and have higher incomes overall than non-stock owners. This may be at least in part circular reasoning: Wealthier people own more of everything, including stocks, so this is no surprise. Suffice it to say that there are far fewer wealthy people who got there by owning bonds, savings accounts, or CDs, than by owning stocks. The wealthiest people in America known by names like Gates, Buffett, Walton, Ellison, Bloomberg, Brin, Dell, Zuckerberg, and so forth—none of them would have made it without the value of their rising stocks.

It is difficult to know why wealthy people own stocks and non-wealthy people do not. Is it a leading or coincident indicator of wealth? How many of these people are wealthy because they *invested* in stocks versus being wealthy just because they *have* stocks? It is probably both, but it certainly does not help those with lesser education when politicians rail against Wall Street, the stock market, and its supposed evils, especially since politicians themselves likely achieved their own wealth through stock investments than through savings accounts and low-yielding bonds.

When I asked Jimmy Bradford, son of the founder of J.C. Bradford & Co., and responsible for building the nation's largest regional brokerage house, what wealthy people have that non-wealthy people do not have, he told me: *"I have met a lot of wealthy people in my day, and the one thing they have in common is money."*[24] In the next chapter, I will discuss what else wealthy investors have in common besides money.

Why Do Stocks Outperform Bonds?

Why stocks outperform bonds is an important question. If you accept conventional thinking that stocks outperform bonds because they are riskier, you would have to discard my premise that risk does not equal reward.

There are two major well-accepted theories that attempt to explain why stocks tend to go up more than bonds in the long term:

1. The equity risk premium.

2. The marginal utility argument.

Both could generally fall under the general heading of risk = reward.

The equity risk premium argument says that stocks will return some combination of the *risk-free* rate of return (usually Treasury notes) plus a premium. The premium is the added return that an investor should demand for holding a risky investment. From this premise come many formulas that express this relationship. The formulas are ultimately what everyone is after, because if you can take a combination of variables like dividend rates, current stock prices, coefficients of relative risk aversions, earnings per share estimates, and so forth, you can come up with smart-looking equations like this one:

$$E_t[r_{t,t+1}] + \text{½var}_t(r_{t,t+1}) - \gamma\text{cov}_t(\Delta \ln C_{t+1}, r_{t,t+1}) = 0$$

And if you can solve equations like this you might either 1) pass the Certified Financial Analysts (CFA) exam, or 2) outperform the stock market. Note I said *or*, not *and*. Why? Because passing the CFA exam and outperforming the stock market do not appear to be positively correlated. This is because stocks, rascals that they are, don't do what the formulas say that they should do. Much like the weather, oil dispersions from underwater gushers, and the fallout from nuclear blasts, stock prices do not behave the way that the models expect. The models have an expected rate of return for stocks, but stocks don't.

Models like this assume very limited variables. Unfortunately, we do not work in the vacuum of frictionless space in the investment world. The friction in our models is other investors' buying patterns, company decisions to discontinue dividends, politicians' unpredictable taxes and interest rate policies, foreign market movements, recessions, and a hundred other unmanageable variables. This is why you have probably never depended on or heard of the equity risk premium theory in your investing life. It just doesn't work too well.

The other argument that seeks to explain stock movement is conceptual, but there are plenty of formulas for it, too. It is called *marginal utility*. Jonathan A. Parker, international programs professor of management at MIT Sloan School of Management, gave me an elegant description of marginal utility:

The marginal utility idea is the main idea in academic finance, and goes back a long way. What you value is an asset that pays off when you are "hungry." For example, in house insurance, you take at a negative average return, because it pays off when you really need it, when your house burns to the ground. The stock market goes down in recessions, when unemployment risk is high, so it loses money at a time most people need more money, so stocks have to pay (on average) more than less "risky" assets to get people to hold them.[25]

There is much logic wrapped around these theories, so I dare not belittle them, but I disagree with both. Anyone who saw what happened to the stock market after March 2009, when it bottomed out, also saw the stock market double during the so called Great Recession (in opposition to marginal utility) exactly when investors needed it.

After a business lifetime of research and experience it seems odd to say that stocks outperform bonds just because they are riskier. None of my numbers would bear this theory out. One imagines a white-bearded celestial purser who rewards us down on earth for taking otherworldly risks with our money. That would be noble, and most fair, but I am skeptical. I have found no tangible proof of such an invisible beneficent market arbiter. I believe in the "invisible hand" of economic theory but not the "invisible hand-out" of market theory. Such thinking (or hoping) is not economics, despite the formulaic approach that these arguments take. Rather, it is therapy, astrology, or even theology when you proffer *Since you are willing to take greater risks, you will be rewarded with higher returns.* At its worst it's foolhardy, like believing that if you drive without your seatbelt (take a risk) you will reach your destination faster (increase your returns). What beyond karma could be driving stock prices?

What's the Real Reason Why Stocks Outperform Bonds?

There is, though, a sensible reason why stocks would outperform bonds. I believe the reason why stocks outperform bonds is this: They *must* in a growing economy. Think of it this way: Bonds are loans. A company's first relationship with financiers is usually through lenders. How does the company eventually pay off this debt? By securitizing its assets in some form, either by private or public equity. New businesses generally borrow first and sell shares next, if they are successful. Investors invest in the company in hopes that it will grow at some marginally greater rate than the annual debt load. In modern growing economies, on average, companies do this. This is the core reason why stocks outperform bonds. It is *not* because they are riskier.

Figure 2-7 may help to illustrate this. You can see that we are mostly a debtor nation (the lighter bars). The darker bars are the equity capital (stocks). If stocks underperformed bonds, the debt would never be paid off. The corollary is that if debt is never paid off, eventually even the stock value drops and finally disappears into bankruptcy.

Perhaps the relationship between bond returns and equity (equity and stock are terms often used interchangeably) returns is easier to see on the downside because as struggling companies begin to miss their payments to bond holders, stock prices begin to fall rapidly. The sub-prime mortgage crisis of 2008 and 2009 was called a *liquidity* crisis. Every financial crisis is a liquidity crisis, and stock returns inexorably rise or fall in the shadow of bond returns.

Public Debt and Equity Capital Raised, 2009–2012 ($billions)[26]

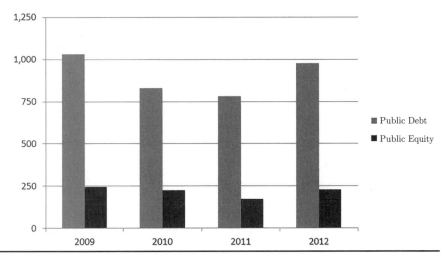

Figure 2-7

Economist Hyman P. Minsky believed that occasional liquidity crises were built into the financial structure and were a result of the banking system degrading from *hedged* finance (banks have sufficient current assets to pay interest), to *speculative* finance (banks can only pay by rolling over debt), and finally to *Ponzi units,* in which banks must sell assets or borrow to pay current debt. This "financial instability hypothesis is a model of a capitalist economy which does not rely upon exogenous shocks to generate business cycles of varying severity."[27] Minsky believed this is natural and built into the system to relieve excesses.

Here is how to think about this relationship between stocks and bonds on a personal level: If you borrow $50,000 from your father for five years at a 6% rate, your interest costs will be $3,000 ($50,000 × 6%) per year. To grow your business you must make more than $3,000 yearly, because first you have to pay back your father. The $50,000 represents a loan (or bond) with your father, and the growth of your business represents your company's value (or stock). Your company value *must* grow at a higher rate than your debt; your stock must return more than your bond. This is a simple way to put it, but I believe a more logical rationale for the higher rates of returns for stocks over bonds, because it addresses what really happens, not what should happen if a tidy formula or hopeful philosophy works.

Supporting my thesis, Ben Inker, portfolio manager and director of asset allocation for GMO (Grantham, Mayo, Van Otterloo & Co), said, "Earnings growth does not fall as manna from heaven. Instead, it is the result of corporate investment, and the return on that investment, in the long run, is fundamentally bound to the cost of capital."[28] Stock returns, too, are bound to the cost of capital.

Stocks have to outperform bonds or companies cannot grow. Now, companies certainly do not have to grow. When they do not it is often because they have too much debt. The value of the business must increase more than the debt service or the company cannot grow. We do not see the opposite very often to provide a negative example because those companies that do not grow faster than their debt disappear.

The *cost* of capital and the *growth* of capital are inextricably linked. What is interesting about the yield on bonds and the return on stocks is how patterned they tend to be. We assume that stock returns are wildly unpredictable and inversely related to bond returns.

However, this is what you see in Figure 2-8 (see page 74) of a comparison between yearly stock returns to yearly bond returns and what should form in your mind when you think about the relationship. Note how returns are within a narrow range from the original $10,000 investment and that on average stocks (the value of the business; the lighter bars) generally out-returned bonds (the cost of capital; the darker bars). I call this the "Capital Cost Premium" because this is the excess return required to pay off the underlying debt. I believe this is a more reasonable explanation and description for what most people know as the "risk" premium. This might be more than you want to know, but it is not more than you should know. The distinction between my view of why stocks go up versus the industry's accepted belief is important or you revert back to the risk = reward myth.

Also note that the bars are roughly proportional, which should not be a surprise. Generally, the lower the cost of capital, the lower the return for stocks. This makes sense. Why should equity returns be wildly disproportionate to bond returns, as they are interconnected stages in the financing of businesses? I have compared bonds that are most like stocks in their return profiles and the way they are priced in the market—high-yield corporate bonds—over one-year periods.

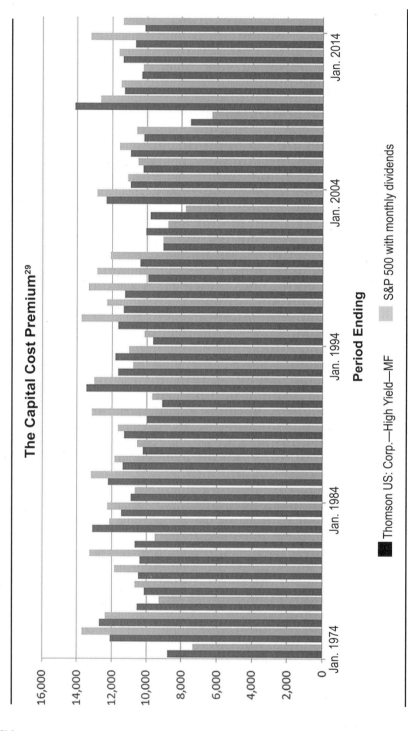

The Capital Cost Premium[29]

Period Ending

■ Thomson US: Corp.—High Yield—MF   S&P 500 with monthly dividends

Figure 2-8

(When you use 10 years or more rolling periods the compounding effect of stocks distorts the annual returns.)

Equity, then, when seen through this perspective is simply a cheaper source of capital than bonds. Therefore, when someone forces me to predict what stocks are going to do, my answer is simply *more than bonds.*

There may be a more academic explanation for this relationship of bond yields and stock prices if you compare my proposition with what is called the Gibson Paradox. The Gibson Paradox, named for economist Alfred Herbert Gibson, asserts that there is a positive correlation between interest rates and general price levels. John Maynard Keynes called Gibson's Paradox "one of the most completely established empirical facts in the whole field of quantitative economics."[30] The discussion of this theory is beyond the scope of this text; I only mention it to say that I am not breaking established economic law by proposing that there is a natural relationship between interest rates and stock prices, or by presuming that one follows the other in kind. Otherwise, we are consigned to the fallacy that superior stock returns are simply a highly theoretical compensator for risk.

PLAN

~

Seek Lower Returns

Reducing Losses Is More Important Than Increasing Returns

"For in the average human
house there is one hole by
which money comes in
and a hundred by which
it goes out."
—G. K. Chesterton

Math is against you. Saying so reminds me of a story.

It was 6:00 on a cold December morning in 1996. We were taking I-40 East out of Nashville and looking directly into the pink glow of the rising sun. My old high school buddy and business partner, Ben Doochin, and I were traveling to sell a 401(k) plan. We passed a cattle truck (there are as many cattle trucks in Tennessee as taxi cabs in Manhattan) and I could see the bulls blowing smoke through the rails of the trailer. It looked like the Chicago Bears' defensive line snorting through their helmets at Soldier Field. I said, "Ben, look at that truck. It's 6:00 in the morning, 10 degrees wind chill, and those poor cows are heading down the road in an open trailer, freezing their tails off." Ben turned to me with one eye on the truck and one eye on me and muttered, "It gets worse."

The Perils of Math

It gets worse. Same with the markets. What do I mean? Let's do a little math quiz. If you lose 25% in year one, what do you have to earn in year two just to break even? Did you say 25%? You would be wrong. You have to make 33% just to break even. That is, you have to find an investment that returns 33% in one year just to get your money back. As a reference, stocks have retuned more than 33% only nine times in the last 86 years (S&P 500 through December 31, 2014). It doesn't take an education in higher math to understand this simple fact: Because you lost money in year one, you are starting with a lower number in year two. You will need

What Goes Down Comes Back Slowly

$10,000 Investment	Return	Value
If you lose...	–25%	$7,500
...you have to make	33.5%	$10,000 to break even

$10,000 Investment	Return	Value
If you lose...	–50%	$5,000
...you have to make	100%	$10,000 to break even

Figure 3-1

a higher return on this lower number than what you lost to break even. What if you lose 50%? If you lose 50% you will have to earn 100% in the next year just to break even. Stocks have never gone up 100% in one calendar year. (See Figure 3-1 on page 80.)

As famed money manager Shelby Cullom Davis, who turned $100,000 into $800,000,000 from 1947 to 1994, said, "You make most of your money in a bear market; you just don't realize it at the time."[1]

It Gets Even Worse

William Lyon Phelps wrote, "If at first you don't succeed, find out if the loser gets anything."[2] Losses don't make you a loser, big losses do. The key is to keep big losses from happening.

This unfortunate reality of how tough it is to make up for large losses is more than a math problem and affects more than just single-year returns. The following charts may look deceptive to you. I have shown them to experienced financial advisors and investors who at first do not believe them. Nonetheless they are vital to our understanding.

We'll start with a question: Would you rather earn a 14% return or an 11.75% return? Naturally you will answer 14%. And naturally this is a trick question. In fact the correct answer may be 14% or it may be 11.75%, thus the best answer is *it depends.* It depends on the composition of those returns. Study carefully the hypothetical portfolio in Figure 3-2.

Would You Rather Get a 14% Return or 11.75% Return?

$10,000 investment =

	Volatile Investment		Stable Investment	
	27.00%	$12,700	11.75%	$11,175
	−13.00%	$11,049	11.75%	$12,488
	30.00%	$14,364	11.75%	$13,955
	−12.00%	$12,640	11.75%	$15,595
	45.00%	$18,328	11.75%	$17,428
	−20.00%	$14,662	11.75%	$19,475
	32.00%	$19,354	11.75%	$21,764
	0.00%	$19,354	11.75%	$24,321
	43.00%	$27,677	11.75%	$27,179
	8.00%	$29,891	11.75%	$30,372
Average	14.00%		11.75%	
GEO Average	11.57%		11.75%	

Returns are not guaranteed and do not represent any particular investments. A diversified portfolio does not guarantee a higher return or lower risk.

Figure 3-2

The first investment of $10,000 averaged a 14% annual return and accumulated $29,891 over 10 years. The second investment averaged 11.75% annual return and accumulated $30,372 over 10 years. How can this be? How can an 11.75% average annual return beat a 14% return? The geometric average (which calculates the compounded return), of course, is lower because the net returns were less. What happened is that even though the average return is higher, the 14% portfolio never recovered from multiple double-digit losses. This is why the geometric average and the net returns are lower.

Note the three losses of 13%, 12%, and 20%. Even with the sizable gains of 27%, 30%, 45%, 32%, and 43% from this volatile portfolio, and the superior 14% average annual return, it underperformed the more stable and lower arithmetic average returning investment.

Understanding the math of investing is vital. Science fiction author Arthur C. Clarke said, "In today's world, 'innumeracy' is an even greater danger than illiteracy, and is perhaps even more common."[3] Additionally, according to estimates, 90 million American adults have trouble reading; yet 110 million have trouble with basic math.[4] Consequently Michael S. Finke and Sandra J. Huston conclude, "Financial literacy in the United States is surprisingly low, and certainly too low to expect that consumers can make effective financial decisions with many of the most complex product markets."[5]

What About the Real World?

Was the last example a trick—the 14% versus 11.75% comparison? Are there any real examples? In other words, are there any actual funds that have had a higher average annual return but, because of the composition of the returns, lower ending values? Yes, there are many examples. Figure 3-3 on page 84 shows one.

This is a comparison of two mutual funds. The first fund had an average yearly return of 10.33%. The second fund had an average yearly return of 14.13%. The fund names do not matter, except to say that these are real funds and actual returns. I could find many comparisons much like this; these are not aberrations. Even so, the first fund, with a *lower* average annual return, outperformed the second fund. Again the internal rate of return, or total return, as measured by the geometric average ("Geo Avg") was higher for the first fund.

Would You Rather Get a 14.13% Return or a 10.33% Return?[6]

$10,000 investment =

Year	Fund A		Fund B	
	Return	Value	Return	Value
1	1.25%	$10,125	−6.89%	$9,311
2	−0.61%	$10,063	10.73%	$10,309
3	−1.53%	$9,909	97.91%	$20,403
4	20.47%	$11,937	46.58%	$29,908
5	17.70%	$14,050	−20.48%	$23,783
6	−5.96%	$13,212	−42.48%	$13,680
7	29.58%	$17,120	43.55%	$19,637
8	25.30%	$21,452	11.95%	$21,985
9	10.90%	$23,791	5.55%	$23,206
10	16.35%	$27,681	5.03%	$24,373
11	0.22%	$27,743	3.95%	$25,336
Average	10.33%		14.13%	
GEO Avg	11.36%		10.51%	

Figure 3-3

The simple fact is this: Year over year, on average, the *outperforming* fund had a lower average return. I'll ask you a simple question: Would you rather own a fund that has a higher average annual return or lower average annual return? Most would answer *a higher annual return* and would prefer fund #2 on the face of it. But remember that you would not necessarily be right making this deceptive choice. What made the lower arithmetic return fund have a higher geometric return? Smaller losses. Remember: If you lose 25%, you need to earn 33% to break even. Losses disproportionately lower returns more than gains raise returns. Losses are hidden wealth destroyers.

What do I mean when I say *losses disproportionately lower returns more than gains raise returns?* We might ask this differently. Would you rather earn 4% per year more return in *up* years or a 4% more return in *down* years? In other words, would you rather do better in good years or in bad years? Think about the question and don't rush to answer. Because most people talk in positive returns (*I beat the market, My fund outperformed your fund,* etc.) they would immediately choose the first answer. They tend to overlook bad years and focus their attention on good years. The problem is that because we never know whether the year ahead will be positive or negative it is essential to have an all-weather investment philosophy where you participate in up years and survive down years. This is important and perhaps the most important lesson in this book.

When 4% Does Not Equal 4%

In this simple example we can see the difference in returns between earning the extra 4% in good years or bad years. (See Figure 3-4 shown on page 86.) Keep in the back of your mind, while you view this chart: *Lose 50%, need to make 100% to break even.* Assume a $100,000 investment for 10 years. In column one the investment earns 10% per year for five years, then –10% per year for the next five years. The loss for the 10-year period is about $5,000. This is another reminder that, despite the fact that we have five +10% years followed by five –10% years, pluses and minuses are not equal in the investing world.

It Is Better to Reduce Risk Than to Increase Returns

$100,000 investment =

Year	Return	Value	Increase Return		Reduce Risk	
				Value		Value
1	–10%	$90,000	–10%	$90,000	–6%	$94,000
2	–10%	$81,000	–10%	$81,000	–6%	$88,360
3	–10%	$72,900	–10%	$72,900	–6%	$83,058
4	–10%	$65,610	–10%	$65,610	–6%	$78,075
5	–10%	$59,049	–10%	$59,049	–6%	$73,390
6	10%	$64,954	14%	$67,316	10%	$80,729
7	10%	$71,449	14%	$76,740	10%	$88,802
8	10%	$78,594	14%	$87,484	10%	$97,683
9	10%	$86,454	14%	$99,731	10%	$107,451
10	10%	$95,099	14%	$113,694	10%	$118,196
Average	0%		2%		2%	
GEO Avg	–0.50%		1.29%		1.69%	

Increase returns = adding 4% to the positive years

Reduce risk = adding 4% to the negative years

Figure 3-4

In column two we added 4% yearly to the positive years (for a total of 14% yearly) and left the negative years at –10% yearly. At the end of 10 years you made $13,694. In column three we left the positive years at +10% yearly, but added 4%

to the negative years (or –6% yearly). After 10 years, with these returns you earned $18,196. Do you see the difference that 4% has made when it is *reducing* your loss instead of *increasing* your gains? $118,196 vs. $113,694. It is the same 4%, but it behaves significantly differently when it is doing the work in bad years rather than in good years. This is what I mean when I say to make more money seek lower returns.

This can be baffling because the average returns in the "Increase returns" and "Reduce risk" columns are both 2%. Despite the average returns being equal, the geometric returns are higher when we reduce risk. The total returns on your investment are 13.69% when we increase returns but 18.20% when we reduce risk. This is why it is often better to reduce risk than it is to increase return. We will talk about how you might achieve this in a coming chapter, but here's a hint: diversify.

If you want to blame anyone for this confusion, blame your seventh-grade math teacher. In seventh grade we learned about *absolute values.* We learned that the absolute value of (4) is +4. The idea for the student is simply to think of numbers in relation to 0. And though it is true that (4) is exactly the same distance from 0 that +4 is, as you can see with your portfolio, being on the south side of 0 is worse than being on the north side of 0. They are not equal, just like risk ≠ reward. Why? They are only equal if you invested for one year. When you invest over one year we don't get returns on the investment we started with; we get returns on the investment *we are left with.*

Did you ever run track? If you are behind after the first five laps it is practically impossible to catch up in the next five laps. In fact the leader can actually slow down and still win.

Investing is the same. If you invest $100,000, then lose 10% the first year, you start year two with $90,000 to invest. If you earn 10% the second year, it is on the reduced amount of $90,000, or $9,000, not on your original $100,000. I have seen this firsthand. When I first got into the business I didn't understand this very deeply. I think my clients and I were both a little baffled by how we could lose 10%, then earn 10%, and have less money! This is why negative returns are hidden wealth destroyers.

Could I Increase My Returns by Lowering My Risk?

We have seen how lower mathematical averages can equal greater investment returns. Can this work for risk, too? That is, could you possibly get higher returns if you lower your risk? What is risk in investment terms? The investment industry uses the expressions *beta* and *standard deviation* to measure relative risk. The higher the beta and standard deviation, the higher the risk, or volatility. So, if risk = reward (as is commonly accepted—but often wrong, as we have seen), then we would expect higher beta and standard deviation to equal higher returns. Do they? Not necessarily.

Look at Figure 3-5 shown on page 89 and Figure 3-6 on page 91. For large growth equity funds and large value equity funds (the two major categories of stock mutual funds), the higher the beta and standard deviation, the *lower* the returns.

Simply put, the higher the risk, the lower the returns. This is opposite of what we would find if risk = reward. Note that there are exceptions to this. There are mutual fund categories and periods that would contradict this, but it is simply inaccurate to say that higher beta and standard deviation automatically equals higher returns.

Lower Beta = Higher Returns[7]

---

902 Large Value Funds

Average *beta* 1.01

beta > average = 6.82% return

beta < average = 7.56% return (lower risk)

147 Small Growth Funds

Average *beta* 1.20

beta > average = 9.22% return

beta < average = 9.67% return (lower risk)

Figure 3-5

Additional supporting evidence came from a recent study that contradicted what we all think we know about risk and reward to conclude: "Over the past 41 years (1968–2008), high volatility and high beta stocks have substantially underperformed low volatility and low beta stocks in U.S. markets."[8]

So the answer is *yes.* You could actually increase your returns by lowering your risk. I say *could* for a reason. The science of investing, what of it there is, is based on formulas, and expected results. Beta and standard deviation are formulas. However, real-world results—that is, what really happens—are based on more than formulas. Actual results are based on multiple inputs, conditions, timing, variances, accidents, and many other factors that are not found in simple formulas. So there will be times when higher beta and higher standard deviation result in higher returns. The message is that now we know that there are many counter examples to the accepted beliefs in the investment industry that higher returns are a natural result of higher risk or higher average annual returns.

Another example of investment industry bias is the way mutual funds are advertised. In a bull market you'll find page after page of advertisements of how well this or that fund manager has done with five-star ratings to prove it. Where were these managers in the bear markets—when it really counted? Where are the advertisements showing where they have demonstrated the value that they are adding to clients by producing smaller losses? Remember: Smaller losses, not bigger gains, are the key.

Increasing Returns While Reducing Risk

Here is another smaller losses story:

Consider an individual who retired in 1973 with a $500,000 portfolio, withdrew 5% of that nest egg in the first year of retirement and increased the withdrawals annually to keep pace with inflation. If that investor put all his money in the S&P 500 stock index, the average annual return through 1990 would be 11.3%, but he would run out of money in that year, according to Franklin Templeton Investments. If the same investor put half his money in stocks and half in bonds, he would still have nearly $100,000 left in 1992, though he received a lower 10.5% average annual return. The stock-and-bond portfolio has only about half the volatility of the all-stock portfolio, "and that's why it's more successful," says Gail Buckner, retirement specialist at Franklin Templeton.[9]

Increasing Returns While Reducing Risk?[10]

$500,000 investment =

Year	100% Stocks 11.3% Return	50% Stocks/50% Bonds 10.5% Return	5% + Inflation Adjusted
1973	$25,000.00	$25,000.00	W
///	$$	$$	I
///	$$	$$	T
///	$$	$$	H
///	$$	$$	D
///	$$	$$	R
///	$$	$$	A
1990	Out of money	$$	W
1991		$$	A
1992		$100,000 remaining	L
1993		$$	S

Figure 3-6

"Higher Risk Merely Generates Higher Volatility"

This section title is a direct quote from investment writer and money manager Eric Falkenstein, PhD. Dr. Falkenstein has done some of the most comprehensive research in the narrow but vitally important field of low-volatility investing. He is an entertaining writer. This is a list of some of his findings;[11] in each case notice that the lower risk alternative outperformed:

- Volatility and returns are inversely related.
- Low beta stocks outperformed high beta stocks.
- High rated (e.g., Moody's and S&P) stocks outperformed low rated stocks.
- Lower leveraged companies outperformed higher leverage companies.
- Blue chip stocks outperformed penny stocks.
- Lower-risk, in the money, call options outperformed higher risk, out of the money, call options.
- Secondary (existing) stocks outperformed initial public offerings.
- The S&P 500 outperformed private equity.
- Investment-grade bonds outperformed high yield bonds.

And...

- Low odds horses tend to beat high odds horses.

- Lottery scratch-off bets beat Powerballs.

- G-rated movies make more money than R-rated movies.

Of course, lower-volatility investing does not always yield higher returns. However, there are enough real-world examples to suggest that continuing to believe that risk = reward is simply contrary to evidence.

The Stock Market Does Not Like Risk

Far from the established meme that the stock market is a blackjack table, in fact the opposite is true: The market abhors risk. Don't forget that the daily stock market close is a 100% accurate measure of the immediate desires of investors. When prices rocket up and down, it indicates nervousness and fear. Eventually investors retreat from this unwanted danger. When they do prices drop.

Proof? Look at how the stock market compares with the "volatility index." The Chicago Board Options Exchange (CBOE) Market Volatility Index (known as the "VIX") was developed by Professor Robert E. Whaley of Vanderbilt University. The VIX is basically a basket of put and call options on the S&P 500. Thus it measures expected future stock price variances or movements. It is also casually known as the *fear index*. Figure 3-7 shows five years through October 31, 2014. The top line (going up) is the S&P 500, and the bottom line (going down) is the VIX. Notice that generally volatility and returns move in opposite directions.

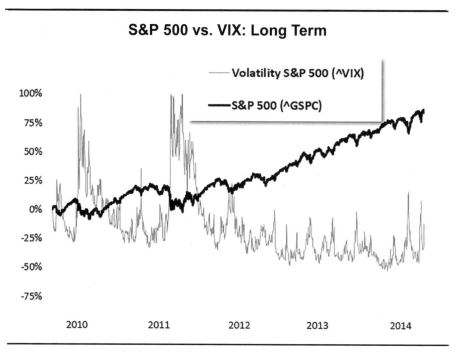

S&P 500 vs. VIX: Long Term

Figure 3-7

If it is difficult for you to see the opposing forces in this five-year period perhaps the charts in Figure 3-8 will be more obvious. This again is the S&P 500 against the VIX but for only the three-month period between June 30, 2014, and September 30, 2014. Note that the returns are mirror opposites: volatility up = market down, and volatility down = market up.

There is a simple equation for these charts: risk ≠ reward.

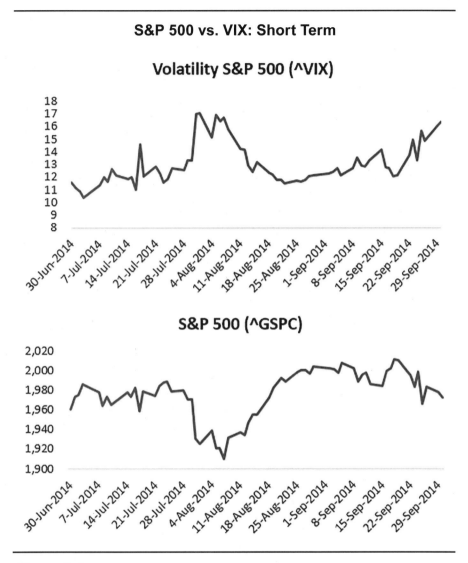

Figure 3-8

Composition of Returns Matters

One reason why I am not a speculative investor with my money or, more importantly, my clients' money is that the higher the attempted return the manager shoots for, the less consistent will be the return. Getting a stray 45% return on your portfolio is not the boon you think it is if you are down 36% the next year, get a 0% rate of return the next year, and so forth. I am not aiming here for some sense of order or predictability; I am only focusing on the math: Consistency yields higher returns. This bias of mine is how I avoided the tech bubble with my clients in the late 90s. I did not believe that 80% returns could continue. I was right and my clients survived it better than the storm chasers and thrill seekers who thought that 80% per year was the new normal.

To help my clients understand the importance of consistency I enjoy asking the following question: *Would you rather get a 15% return or a 15% return on your money?* The half-confused, half-annoyed look of exasperation is worth asking the question. More importantly, it forces my clients to start thinking of returns differently. For example, would you prefer a 30% return the first year on your investments and a 0% return the second year, or would you prefer a 15% return the first year and a 15% return the second year? It doesn't really matter, does it? Either way your average return is 15%, right? Wrong. Actually it does matter. And it matters for the same reason that you should attempt to make your losses smaller rather than your gains bigger.

If you make 30% in year one and 0% in year two you will make less than if you had earned 15% yearly for two years. Why? Because with the investment where you earned 15% in both years, in the second year the 15% is made on the 15% that you have *already earned*. So you have a *compounding* effect. (See Figure 3-9.)

Would You Rather Get a 15% Return or a 15% Return?

Inconsistent Returns

$10,000 investment	Return	Value
	30%	$13,000 1st year
	0%	**$13,000** 2nd year
Average return:	15%	

Consistent Returns

$10,000 investment	Return	Value
	15%	$11,500 1st year
	15%	**$13,225** 2nd year
Average return:	15%	

Figure 3-9

Compounding is not the same as adding. A definition of *compound* is "to pay (interest) on both the accrued interest and the principal." Synonyms for *compound* are *accelerate, boost,* and *amplify.* Synonyms for *add* are *join, unite,* and *append.* See the difference? I do not mean for this to turn into Scrabble, but I do mean for you to see the relative value of compounding.

An analogy is body composition. If someone asked you if a 220-pound or 170-pound man was healthier, I would hope that you would ask some follow-up questions, such as:

- How tall are the two men?
- What are their body mass indexes?

- What are their relative cholesterol levels?

- What about blood pressure, etc.?

The true picture of one's physical health and the health of his or her portfolio are in the composition; 220 and 170 are irrelevant numbers.

Still don't believe that losses affect performance more than gains? Here's a quiz. Which 10-year period in the stock market had an average annual return during the positive years of *15.4%*, the fourth-longest *positive* run in history, and cumulative positive years that were 12% higher than the negative years? Answer: the decade that ended December 31, 2009. What else do we know about this decade? Per the *Wall Street Journal*, "In nearly 200 years of recorded stock-market history no calendar decade has seen such a dismal performance as the 2000s."[12] What I did not mention is that for the same 10-year period the market suffered four negative years. In other words, the four negative years for this 10-year period were enough to turn it into the *worst decade ever*. Are you starting to see this?

The key is to begin to look at risk differently than perhaps you ever have, and to understand that to enjoy above-average long-term returns you need to focus on having smaller losses, instead of bigger gains. Too often investors only talk in terms of positive returns. They will say something along the lines of *I expect to make between 10 and 12% long term*. They really should say, *I rarely expect to lose between 10 and 12% because it takes too long to make up the loss, and losses affect returns more than gains.*

You have to be careful not to take the wrong lesson from all of this. The lesson is not to run from the stock markets. In fact, none of this works if you put all of your money in CDs and money market funds. We will see later that the key is to stay invested. Turning risk into reward, the benefits of compounding, and higher returns, come from diversifying within the markets, not surrendering from the markets.

Here are the refrigerator magnet reminders. *Losses affect performance more than gains. Pay attention to the minuses and the pluses will take care of themselves.* Or, as author Dr. Craig Israelsen wrote, *"The best way to grow and protect wealth is to avoid large losses."*[13]

I mean it when I say to make more money seek lower returns. I think you know now how I mean that. If you want to brag about your investing acumen, brag about how you outperformed in a bad market, not how you did in a strong market. In baseball, winning is better than losing. In investing, not losing is better than winning.

Think Long Term, Act Long Term

What else is important to boost your returns? If I asked you if you are a long-term investor or a short-term investor, you would likely respond that you are a long-term investor. However, as the saying goes, you are what you do. Do investors generally think long term? Let's look at history. "In the last decade the amount of time that investors kept funds dropped to an average of three years from ten.... (However) the Financial Research Corp findings support the case against performance chasing. The study found that investors who held funds for just three years in the 1990s had a 20 percent lower return than if they stuck with their holdings for 10 years."[14] So, not only are investors by some measure holding mutual funds for less time, their returns suffer for it. Here's an example: According to Peter Lynch, three-fourths of all investors who invested in Fidelity Magellan lost money. This is because they traded in and out instead of just leaving it alone.

Long-term investors generally beat short-term traders. There appears to be a culture gap between long-term investors and short-term traders, as in this humorous analysis from writer Andy Kessler about a hedge fund manager who, "[i]f he had ever had a long-term gain it's because he forgot to sell something."[15]

The 1990s were a particularly fruitful decade where U.S. stock returns performed at almost twice their historical average. It is also the decade that boasts the longest winning track record for the Dow Jones Industrial Average with an astounding nine years of consecutive positive returns (1991–1999), which has never been matched before or after. Unfortunately, you wouldn't have known that at the beginning of the decade. The long-term investor who ignored the recession, high interest rates, and the 1990 oil price shock after Iraq invaded Kuwait was well rewarded.

However, if you tried to outwit the market during this period by trading in and out of it (as a few of my clients tried to do) you would not have been rewarded. From August 1997 the S&P 500 returned 88% over the next 10 years. Had you missed just the best 20 days in that 10-year period your gain would have turned into a 20% loss.[16]

Why the focus on long term? "History shows that the vast majority of the time, the stock market does next to nothing. Then, when no one expects it, the market delivers a giant gain or loss—and promptly lapses back into its usual stupor," says Javier Estrada, PhD, a finance professor at IESE Business School in Barcelona, Spain, who has studied the daily returns of the Dow Jones Industrial Average from 1900.[17] *Wall Street Journal* writer Jason Zweig asked him to extend his research through the end of 2008. Professor Estrada found that if you took away the 10 best days, two-thirds of the cumulative gains produced by the Dow over the past 109 years would disappear. Conversely, had you sidestepped the market's 10 worst days, you would have tripled the actual return of the Dow. "Although we could make a bundle of money if we could accurately predict those good and bad days," says Professor Estrada, "the sad truth is that we're very, very unlikely to do that." The moments that made all the difference were just 0.03% of history: 10 days out of 29,694.[18]

The Dow went up 37% in 1995, the best year I had ever seen. Brokers are the opposite of investors: We don't sell when stocks go down—which is good. Instead we sell when stocks go up—which is bad. We do a good job keeping our clients in the market during catastrophic times because we know that history is on our side and the markets will recover. But we think (wrongly) that our value add is selling at the top, before the market starts to slide. I think some of us do this just to show clients that we are slightly more in touch with the market than they are. It's a terrible mistake, so as an investor be wary of it and don't sell.

John Templeton had the best trading strategy I ever heard. When I was with Merrill Lynch years ago in Nashville he taught us on a conference call with his sweet Winchester, Tennessee, accent that "the best time to invest is when you have the money, and the best time to sell is when you need the money. Otherwise, leave it alone." This is an expression that he repeated a lot, and for good reason.

I also remember a great American Funds wholesaler that used to call on me named George Truesdail. George was a former FBI agent, an energetic and very pleasant guy. We had just come off this spectacular year in the market, and I told George that I was thinking about trimming client portfolios and sort of hiding in the tall grass of cash for a while to protect them if the market falls. He told me, "Andy, I understand what you are saying and it certainly sounds sensible. I'm tempted to do the same thing myself from time to time, but I don't." I asked him why. "Because, I never know when to buy back." How right George was. Over the next four years the Dow was up 29%, 25%, 18%, and 27%, respectively.

The problem when you sell on a "high" is that you have to decide when to buy back if the market goes higher. And because the market is up 65% of the time you will statistically be forced to buy back at a higher price, which is emotionally very hard to do; or sit and watch the market go up; or simply watch the market make money for everyone but you. I watched a client sit on cash for all of these five years in his retirement plan because he thought he could outsmart the market. He is very bright, an extremely successful businessman, and a savvy real estate investor. But he was acting on an erroneous principle: He thought he could time the market.

Buy and Hold

Let's talk about another important investment maxim. First, think of a farmer. When he plants a tomato seed, how often does he dig it up to see how it's doing? What if he digs it up every day he thinks it won't rain and then re-plants it the day he thinks it will rain? Or what if he digs up the seed to clean off the pesky little sprouts and roots that are growing out of it? He does this every day because he knows that nature can be hard, and he wants to make sure that everything's going well underground. Then around harvest time he stands there and wonders were the crop is. He took such care of the little seed, cleaning it off every day, digging around it, moving it to just the right spot.... See what I mean?

A good farmer would never do this, but this is exactly what some of my clients do. Every day they are checking their portfolio. What's that? Yellen is lowering the Fed Funds rate today? The Hang Seng is down 10%? A Democrat was just elected president? The Dow is off 300 points? None of this matters for the investor. You wouldn't sell your house and move if your neighbor got $10,000 less for his house than his listing price, would you? Be a farmer: Be patient. Leave it alone.

Here is a glaring illustration on why it is better to seek lower returns (buy and hold) than higher returns (beat the market) from a *Wall Street Journal* article:

Just 11 of 81 stock-market timers—those advisers who try to predict when to get into or out of the market to sidestep declines and participate in rallies—actually made money during the bear market that began after the Internet bubble burst in March 2000 and ended in October 2002. These market timers have lost so much since then that, on average, they are in the red over the entire period since March 2000, and having chalked up a 0.8% annualized loss. A simple buy-and-hold approach using the Wilshire 5000 over the same period, by contrast, gained an annualized 4.2%, including reinvested dividends.[19]

And here's more evidence: Warren Buffett's mentor Benjamin Graham said, "The investor's chief problem—even his worst enemy—is likely to be himself."[20] Likewise, writer Chuck Jaffe, in an article titled "You Are Your Portfolio's Worst Enemy," wrote, "It's not a real surprise that the trading investor—the one who gives up on a fund after three years to buy something 'better'—does worse than the one who overcame their disappointment to let the money ride."[21] He refers to a study by the Vanguard Group that analyzed "more than 40 million return paths to cover every possible trade that could have been made among diversified domestic stock funds from 2004 through 2013."[22] The results? The buy-and-hold strategy delivered a 7.1% average annualized return in large-cap growth funds compared to 4.3% for the performance-chasers.

Leave it alone. Or as astronaut Pete Conrad said: "If you don't know what to do, don't do anything."[23]

It's Not Your Equipment; It's You

If you must "do something," learn to do it well, okay? The great golfer Chi Chi Rodriguez recommended that golfers trying to improve their game should play an entire 18 holes with just a five iron. What he was trying to prove was that golf is about mechanics, the approach, the swing, the follow-through, and the finesse, and not about the clubs. Golf is about golfers, not golf clubs. I am a lousy golfer. I like to joke that it is my $100 Dunlop clubs that is keeping me from the PGA tour. I have never seen a great golfer say that they are holding this 25-pound silver trophy because of their Big Bertha driver, but I've seen plenty of weekend gardeners blame their equipment.

The same holds true with investing. This is about you, not any particular magical, "must own" investment. Getting good at investing is a skill that can be learned just like golf. But first you need to realize that the great skill is not predicting the market, it is predicting you. Great investors know who they are; they know their strengths and weaknesses. They are so good that they can predict themselves with great accuracy.

Don't Let the Sham of Consumerism Destroy Your Portfolio

Another investor fallacy is focusing only on costs. Why is the investment industry the only profession where its product seems better the cheaper it is, when there is no correlation between returns and costs? Example: What is the *cheapest* investment? A money market fund. What is the most expensive investment? A hedge fund. What is often the lowest-yielding investment? A money market fund. What is often the highest-returning investment? A hedge fund. Cheap investors get cheap returns.

To illustrate this I compared the cheapest mutual fund and the average mutual fund for 10 years. Guess what? The *cheapest* underperformed the *average* by almost 3% per year. (See Figure 3-10.) Will this always happen? No. But does it make you pause a moment before choosing investments for your future solely on cost? It should.

The *Cheapest* Mutual Fund vs. the *Average* Mutual Fund[24]

The *cheapest* = .86% avg annual return

vs.

The *average* = 3.75% avg annual return

Figure 3-10

American consumers are fickle. How many contradictions can you count here? We want the lowest price, but demand the highest quality. We want immediate service, but are unhappy when we have to deal with inexperienced people. We want lifetime guarantees from the cheapest products. We don't want to have to drive a long way to shop, but are angry when Walmart builds a superstore in our neighborhood. And when we get there, despite the fact that we always buy the same mustard, there are 75 different brands, and 12 different sizes from 1/4-ounce packets to 10-gallon drums. After our mercenary shopping campaign we demand that the manager bow and thank us for our business, upon which his profit margin is 3%.

There is, likewise, a much higher cost to investing incorrectly than there is to paying high fees. This is not to say that there is a tradeoff. There is not. More expensive investment programs do not necessarily lead to greater returns. Nor is the corollary true that cheaper investment programs necessarily lead to higher returns.

Being conscious of fees is not the same as paying the least amount possible for financial services. Just as you wouldn't seek out the cheapest lawyer, doctor, or college for your children, you shouldn't seek the cheapest investment program.

The media is the worst offender. Almost every time that I see a chart of recommended mutual funds in the financial or popular press it is a comparison of "no-load" mutual funds. For some reason (and it certainly isn't financial) writers leave out load funds as if they are automatic losers. You will soon see this is not true. Think of the finish line, not the starting line. What difference does it make if you paid 4½% up-front for a fund that returned more long run, even after the load, than a no-load fund?

There are some financial writers that, as a matter of faulty principle, will not recommend load funds no matter what the returns are. This is senseless. Example: There was a fund from Fidelity that is now closed to new investors. It had a very high sales charge. Despite that it also had startlingly high returns—mostly because of two things: great management and a structure that made investors dollar cost average into it and severely penalize them if they took withdrawals. It was a forced savings plan. It made investors do what they would otherwise not do: buy in down markets and hold for the long term. It was great, it was expensive, and now it's gone. Not good.

Penny Wise, Dollar Foolish

Consumerism is a broken and ultimately expensive dream. It doesn't work at Walmart and it doesn't work on Wall Street. How do I know? If consumerism worked, then Americans would be getting gradually richer. Because of low-cost goods consumers should have been saving money, taking those savings, investing, and growing richer. In fact they are not. The money that they save on 64 ounces of mustard at Walmart does not go into their savings account; it goes into a 64-ounce tub of ketchup. We pay less so we can buy more—not so we can save more.

We bring this doomed philosophy to investing, but low fees do not mean low costs. Sometimes, quite surprisingly, a lifetime of low fees can add up to high costs.

How could this be? I have a client who refused to invest in mutual funds. He simply would not pay anybody a management fee. His thinking was that he could buy the stocks himself (at discounted commissions, of course) and hold them for free in a brokerage account with me. For the amateur investor the only way that this strategy could work is simply by the application of good luck. For 15 years all he held with me was a portfolio of utility stocks. They were solid companies that paid dividends, the very kind of companies that are hard to talk an investor out of. Despite that I tried to talk him out of these stocks for years, but I eventually gave up.

Why did I try to talk him out of these stocks? Because utility stocks act more like bonds than stocks. Public service or utility commissions have used their powers to neutralize the profitability of public utilities (in the name of consumerism, ironically). Consequently utility stocks are quasi-government fixed-income-like instruments. If you look at the return on assets and return on equity of utilities versus the S&P 500, you quickly see that utilities don't measure up. It's not because they aren't good businesses; it is because they have been reduced to protected and severely regulated entities without much hope of significant returns. Most financial advisors know this; most clients do not. One couldn't imagine 20 years ago that the government would have the power or motivation to purposely hold back the profitability of a public company, but it does. The net result has been that public utility common stock now has the risk of a stock but the return of a bond—not the kind of risk/reward tradeoff that savvy investors should accept.

I wanted a client to sell his utilities and invest in a well-managed growth mutual fund. But, here we go: Funds have fees. What has this cost him? Plenty. Utilities have significantly underperformed the Dow Jones Industrial Average for the last 20 years by roughly 2½% per year.[25]

Am I picking on this client? This unfair, right? Undoubtedly he is an unsophisticated person. He earned his PhD in physics from Johns Hopkins and taught college physics for his entire career. You decide. Do you see now how the *avoidance* of fees can be very costly in the long run?

L oad Funds or No-Load Funds?

The point I am driving at it this: There is one other thing you have been taught about investing besides risk = reward, and that is *cheaper is always better.* False. There is no service industry that suffers more from its unschooled hecklers than the investment industry. A day does not pass that a financial writer does not hurl invective at the industry usually under the byline that it fleeces its clients. Most of these columns and books are written by people who have never actually advised anyone on how to invest, nor have they seen the damage that I have to undo as an advisor with their flawed advice.

For example, take no-load funds. There is no such thing as a no-load fund in actuality because all mutual funds charge fees. With no-load funds you just don't see the fees. A load fund, however, charges explicit fees basically in three ways. You may have heard of A, B, and C shares. A shares charge up-front, B shares charge a declining back-end load or surrender charge (depending on how long the shares are kept within the fund family), and C shares charge nothing up-front but a deferred load if redeemed out of the fund family within 12 months. Generally, the internal expenses (not having to do with the load) are higher for B and C shares. No-load funds have no sales charges, but they do have internal expenses—and of course should.

I hope no investor expects to have a professional money manager and an entire back office that perform lots of shareholder services like tax reporting, automatic investing, check writing, 800# customer service, online account services, distributions, valuations, record-keeping, and so forth for free.

What you will quickly see when you view the numbers is that there is little difference between load and no-load funds. Figure 3-11 shows the returns of all load funds and no-load funds that have at least a 15-year track record.

There Is Little Difference Between Load Funds and No-Load Funds[26]

Load Funds	TOTAL	No-Load Funds	TOTAL
Mutual Fund Universe	30,178	Mutual Fund Universe	30,178
Tot Ret Annlzd 15 Yr.	10,012	Tot Ret Annlzd 15 Yr.	7,559
Average returns		Average returns	
Returns 15 yrs.	5.75%	Returns 15 yrs.	5.79%
Returns 10 yrs.	6.64%	Returns 10 yrs.	6.66%
Returns 5 yrs.	10.18%	Returns 5 yrs.	10.06%
Returns 3 yrs.	10.44%	Returns 3 yrs.	10.72%
Returns 1 yr.	14.60%	Returns 1 yr.	14.27%

Figure 3-11

Figure 3-12 compares all load funds from the top five mutual fund companies that charge sales loads (by assets under management) and no-load funds *after* the upfront sales charge has been deducted for a hypothetical $50,000 investment. (The returns would be even higher for load funds with the more money you invest because of break-point pricing.) Note that in many cases even after the sales charge the load funds outperformed. This will surprise every investment industry writer and maybe even you. (I included "turnover rate" to show that no-load funds generally have a higher rate, which is a hidden cost to the shareholder, but is not included in the expense ratio.)

Many Load Funds Beat No-Load Funds Even After Load[27]

Load Funds

Fund Company	# of Distinct Funds	NER	Turnover	Tot Ret % 15-Yr. Annual	Value of $50,000 15 Yrs.
A	45	0.58	52.4	6.4	$113,206
B	116	0.97	70.1	6.2	$111,138
C	382	0.60	63.6	5.7	$104,171
D	125	0.89	34.3	6.3	$112,168
E	73	1.21	53.1	5.8	$104,589

No-Load Funds

Fund Company	# of Distinct Funds	NER	Turnover	Tot Ret % 15-Yr. Annual	Value of $50,000 15 Yrs.
All	4869	0.80	88.3	5.5	$105,805

Figure 3-12

These results would not surprise Morningstar, Inc., which says, "While true no-load funds may be attractive from an expense standpoint, this does not suggest that funds with loads should be shunned. Many funds with consistently above-average track-records have fees and expenses attached."[28]

Certainly there is no proof on cost alone that no-load funds outperform load funds. Therefore, the no-load investor has practically no greater chance of higher performance than the load investor. I would have to concede, however, that if either no-load investors or load investors consistently showed risk-adjusted outperformance 80–90% of the time, then I would be a partisan. But the evidence is not there, and certainly does not justify the financial media continuing to ignore load funds.

What's the point of this discussion? Wouldn't you rather *not* pay a load than pay one? Perhaps, but don't automatically expect higher net returns or lower risk because of it. Advisors can offer load or no-load funds these days, so this is not a matter of preference but principle. It simply is not wise to disregard half of all mutual funds and hundreds of terrific money managers because they carry a sales charge.

Fees vs. Commissions

Advisors charge either fees or commissions. Which should you prefer? As usual the best answer is *it depends.* First I want to inoculate you against the erroneous thinking that fee-based advisors are "on the same side of the table as you" but commission advisors are not. This is false. Commission advisors can definitely be on the same side of the table as you.

Which is preferable depends on the investments you are making, the level of service you expect, the added value that the fee-based planner may bring, and so on. It is vital for you to make the advisor justify his or her fee. As a rule of thumb if you are a long-term buy-and-hold investor, then commissions and loads are a better deal for you than fees. However, if the advisor is doing a lot of extra work that you need such as semi-annual reviews, financial planning, detailed accounting, directly working with your accountant, estate planning, education planning, tactical fund management, and so forth, a fee can be worth it.

Suitability vs. Fiduciary

Associated with the commissions or fees discussion is the question of suitability or fiduciary standards. There is no topic in the investment industry that is more prone to politics, hyperbole, and vague assertions than this one.

Generally, most registered representatives that charge a commission are governed by the suitability standard; most fee-based financial planners are governed by the fiduciary standard. Some regulators, meanwhile, are attempting to do away with the suitability standard and make all advisors, whether commission or fee-based, fiduciaries. The intent is to raise industry standards so investors will be better protected. However, many suspect that this is simply an attempt to increase the legal liability of financial services firms.

The suitability standard as described in FINRA Rule 2111 is comprehensive. It states that advisors must have a reasonable basis for making investment recommendations; that he or she should be able to justify all trades and asset allocation models used; that the recommendations are based on a thorough review of the client's investment objectives, risk tolerance, age, experience, knowledge, and other factors; and that the recommendation must fit the client's financial ability. Further, the advisor must observe basic investment practices, such as diversification, dollar cost averaging, and tax deferred investing (if applicable), and understand historic returns of stocks, bonds, cash and other assets, effects of inflation, and estimates of future retirement income needs. Finally the rule states that it is "not limited to"[29] these criteria, which means that even when the advisor follows these practices he may still be legally liable.

What is a fiduciary? According to the Securities Industry and Financial Markets Association (SIFMA), "A fiduciary relationship is generally viewed as the highest standard of customer care available under law."[30] A fiduciary has a duty to act in the best interest of the customer, and to provide complete disclosure of all facts and conflicts of interest.

I certainly support the aim of the fiduciary but also believe that as an investor you should know that the suitability standard is very protective to you. Regulators and politicians who generalize with the claim that anything but a fiduciary is unsafe to your financial future are simply wrong.

My recommendation would be for you to ask under which standard your advisor acts. If he or she acts under the suitability standard, ask that he or she provides you with a list of potential conflicts of interest and all material facts of any investment recommended (just as do fiduciaries). If the advisor is acting as a fiduciary then ask him or her to state such in writing, and ask that he or she also observes the suitability standard.

If you do this then you can better manage your financial affairs while the investment industry grows out of (hopefully) its identity crisis.

Have You Heard the One About the Brain-Damaged Investor?

Sounds like the start of a joke, but it's not. Let's look at some other ways that you as an investor can make a difference besides understanding load versus no-load funds, fees versus commissions, and suitability versus fiduciary standards.

A study published in the journal *Psychological Science* by a team of researchers from Carnegie Mellon University, the Stanford Graduate School of Business, and the University of Iowa showed that brain damage is good for investment returns. Why? Because, as the study indicated, "Bringing emotion to investing can lead to bad outcomes."[31] Fifteen participants, who had lesions in a region of the brain that controls emotions, and therefore had limited emotional responses such as fear or anxiety, were tested for their investment skill. They had otherwise-normal IQs. The brain-damaged investors outperformed the healthy participants. "They don't react emotionally to things. Good investors can learn to control their emotions in certain ways to become like these people."[32] Fear, however, kept the healthy investors from making obvious good decisions in their self-interest. Emotions can either pull the investor out of the game too early or keep him or her from ever getting in. Or, as Dr. Janet Geringer Woititz said, "The power of being emotionally stuck is far greater than the power of reason."[33] And sometimes, as with investing, that power (or in this case, lack of) is for the good.

Further to the emotional content of investing, according to John Ferry, an Edinburgh, Scotland–based financial writer and a senior correspondent for *Worth,* "Warren Buffett once said that investing is not a game in which the guy with the 160 IQ beats the guy with the 130 IQ. Once you have ordinary intelligence, what you need is the temperament to control the urges that get other people into trouble."[34]

The evidence for the existence of something other than a mathematical model to explain investment behavior is something that I have found ever since I saw my first client sell when others were buying while using the same information. How we process data, and what use or misuse we make of our emotional impulses, has more bearing on investment success than whether you can calculate internal rate of returns or compound interest. As Angela Lee Duckworth said, "Intelligence is really important, but it's still not as important as self-control."[35]

Now That You Know, Know What You Feel

The other part of this behavioral approach has to do with what psychologists call the conative-cognitive divide. That is, we are simple feeling and thinking machines, and we bring that rusty or well-oiled machine to all of our problems.

In my experience, the clients who are either pessimistic or excitable make the worst investors. They make hasty decisions then change their minds. They panic when the market drops and sell. They get overjoyed when the market goes up and buy at the top. Basically, they do all the wrong things. There is an answer for them, which I will discuss later. However, if they (you, if it applies) could take a breath and seek lower returns in the way that I have described in this chapter, I believe they (you) would do a lot better. The next chapter is devoted to you.

Predict Yourself, Not the Stock Market:

Establishing Your Goals Is More Important Than Guessing the Market

> "I can calculate the motions of
> the heavenly bodies but not the
> movements of the stock market."
>
> —Isaac Newton,
> after being wiped out in
> a stock market crash in 1768

Past performance does not predict future returns.

We have all seen this warning. If past performance does not predict future returns, then what *does* predict future returns? You do. Your returns are far more dependent on your *behavior* as an investor than on fund *performance.* Mabel Newcomer, former Vassar economics department professor, and consultant to the U.S. Treasury and International Monetary Fund, had an elegant way of putting it: "Have the courage to stand aside and watch for a little while. It is more important to know where we are going than to get there quickly. Do not mistake activity for achievement."[1]

Jimmy Bradford, whom I spoke of earlier, told me: "I haven't noticed a correlation between knowledge and wealth. It is more about temperament. 90% psychology and make-up and temperament, and 10% do you know what an ETF is."[2] Or, as Don Phillips with Morningstar, Inc., said in reference to the careless belief that investors simply need to blindly buy an index fund, "Indexing does not address behavioral issues."[3]

Is investing failure or success mostly a behavioral problem? Dalbar, Inc., an investment research firm in Boston, calculated the compound annual returns for equities (stocks), fixed income (bonds), and inflation. The stock market did very well during the period from 1994 to 2002, returning 12.2% per year. But, the average investor only received a 2.6% annual return, or 78% *less* than the market.[4] Fixed-income investors did a little better against the index but still significantly underperformed. Additionally, in the declining interest rate environment from 1984 to 2003, bonds were up on average 11.7%. (Whatever bull market there was in stocks over this period it was even bigger in bonds.) Here again investors significantly underperformed and were up only 4.2% on average, or 64% less than the market.[5]

If you doubt the validity of these figures, Dalbar ran the numbers again. From 1986 to 2005 the S&P 500 returned 11.9% yearly and the average equity (stock) investor earned 3.9%. From 1987 to 2007 the S&P 500 Index returned 11.8% yearly and the average equity investor earned just 4.5% yearly.

And if you doubt the validity of *those* numbers, they ran them again: "For the 30 years ending Dec. 31, 2013...equity fund investors earned an average annual return of 3.69% compared with the S&P 500's 11.11%."[6]

If you still doubt these numbers, the Investment Company Institute conducted a similar study. The results are shown in Figure 4-1. Notice the spread between Stock Funds and the S&P 500. Investors underperformed the averages in each period.

Investor Returns Are Often Below the Benchmarks[7]

| | Investor Returns | | Benchmark Returns | |
	Stock Funds	Bond Funds	S&P 500	Barclays Agg.
20 Yrs.	4.3%	1.0%	8.2%	6.3%
10 Yrs.	6.1%	1.2%	7.1%	5.2%
5 Yrs.	–0.8%	1.6%	1.7%	6.0%
3 Yrs.	7.6%	2.9%	10.9%	6.2%
12 Mos.	15.6%	4.7%	16.0%	4.2%

Figure 4-1

Dalbar concluded that *investment return is far more dependent on investment behavior than on fund performance.* Does that surprise you? It shouldn't. Name any success or failure in your life that did not in some tangible way depend on your behavior.

What has been one of the results of this almost unbelievable sub-par performance by investors? Edward N. Wolff, an economist with NYU, told me that 40% of Americans have no financial wealth. That figure did not change between two studied periods between 1998 and 2004, *despite the fact* that the Dow Jones Industrial Average rose 31% over the same period.

Dalbar's advice? "[S]et expectations below market indexes, control exposure to risk, monitor risk tolerance and present forecasts in terms of probabilities."[8] See the word *risk* in there anywhere?

S end in the Clowns

Don't feel bad not knowing where the stock market is going; neither did Sir Isaac Newton. You should be content knowing that you and the person who discovered gravity, built the first reflecting telescope, and was a creator of calculus have something in common.

Worse than *not* knowing where the market is going is *knowing* where the market is going. There is a special name for those who know where the market is going: insider traders. Though there are certain short-term advantages to insider trading, there are few successful long-term insider traders who are known to anyone besides curious fellow prisoners. The financial markets were created so companies can raise capital and so anyone can invest in those companies; they were not designed for gamers and manipulators.

Let's take a look at some of the more laughable recent attempts at predicting the stock market. These are authentic book titles by market experts:[9]

- *Dow 30,000 by 2008! Why it's Different This Time.*
- *Dow 36,000: The New Strategy for Profiting From the Coming Rise in the Stock Market.*
- *Dow 40,000: Strategies for Profiting From the Greatest Bull Market in History.*
- *Dow 100,000: Fact or Fiction.*

Let me help you with the last one: fiction. When you see where the authors' predicted the stock market (in this case the Dow Jones Industrial Average) is headed, I do not argue that one day the market will not reach 30,000, 36,000, 40,000, or even 100,000. One day the market *will* reach 30,000, 36,000, 40,000, and 100,000. In fact, I think I will live to see each—except the last one. My point is that the market has not (for two of the books) and will not (for the other two) reach these levels when they say it will. The math, market history, and expected returns by any reasonable measure do not get there. Each author was wrong. It doesn't keep them from getting published. It may, though, keep you from making money. They remind me of the famed economist who predicted eight of the last five recessions.

We Are at the Top, the Bottom, or the Middle, I Think

Here are more recent attempts at predicting the stock market. "Is it all over for stocks?" sounds the lament from a woeful *Money* magazine writer. He even issues a puzzling defeatist challenge to the reader: "If you haven't second guessed yourself yet, maybe you just aren't paying attention." To add the authoritative urgency to this air raid warning comes Rob Arnott, the formidable star of the indexing world with "we're headed for a depression."[10]

Were the country's most popular consumer finance magazine and the index industry's ranking luminary correct? Yes—for one calendar quarter. Then they were wrong for every quarter after. I think a picture is more compelling than raw numbers. (See Figure 4-2.) Their prediction date is at the left of this chart. Actually, their timing was pretty good. But, what they didn't know was that they had timed the bottom not the top.

The Stock Market Is Dead, 2008

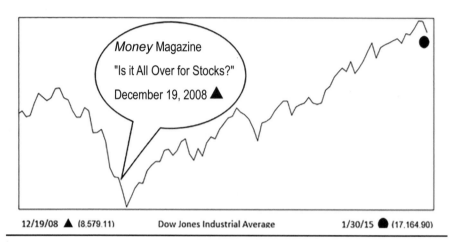

Figure 4-2

Figure 4-3 illustrates another favorite prediction:

The Stock Market Is Dead, 1979

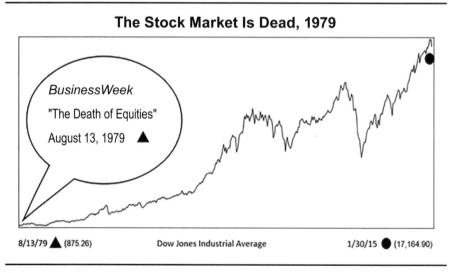

Figure 4-3

For the 34 years, through 2014, after *BusinessWeek*'s headline "The Death of Equities" a dollar invested in stocks would have returned $50, an 11.82% return annually.[11] It would be difficult to find a better investment for that period.

Or, if you cannot pick the top or the bottom, like the market wizards mentioned previously, then pick the top *and* the bottom. The media has discovered a new way to *always* be right. How do you do this? Predict both directions at once. On the same day and same page of a popular investing Website a professional investor named John Hussman predicted an "80% Chance of a Big Market Crash" while *Forbes* columnist and money manager Ken Fisher advertised, "Is Another Bull Market Around the Corner?"[12] Were they both right? Were they both wrong? Amazingly enough, even when they hedged and picked both directions, both were wrong. For the next two years after December 4, 2009, the Dow Jones Industrial Average was up 8% per year, with no bear or bull market in between. How, I wonder, does this help the nervous investor?

Here is another example. I hesitate to pick on the *Wall Street Journal,* because it is among the most authoritative of all investment market publications, but again, this is why they and everyone else should get out of the prediction business.

On December 11 we learn that a recession is coming with this headline: "Economists Say Recession Risk Is Climbing." Then on December 17: "Why Economists Are Betting a Recession Won't Happen." What happened in those fateful six days in which there was a complete reversal of opinion on the most significant of all investment predictions: *Will we* or *will we not* fall into a recession?

On the same day, December 17, the *Wall Street Journal* told us to forget the holidays. The markets are ruining everything in this headline: "Happy Holidays? Not for Financial Markets." By December 22 happy days are here again: "Stocks Deliver Holiday Cheer to Finish Week."

This habit of measuring investor, or perhaps reporter, sentiment one week at a time is an enemy to the long-term investor. If investors followed the headlines they would have bought and sold two times each in this 11-day period. Instead, it would pay to ignore all of the cheer and fear.

So Really, Where Is the Stock Market Going?

So much for the financial media.

Years ago the *Dick Davis Digest* asked Warren Buffett (the greatest living value investor), John Templeton (the dean of international investing), and Peter Lynch (one of the most successful mutual fund managers) the following question: *Where do you believe the stock market is going?* Warren Buffett answered, "We do not have, never have had, and never will have an opinion about where the stock market will be a year from now." Peter Lynch answered, "I have no feeling for the direction of the market over the near term, or the next three to twelve months...." And John Templeton answered, "Ignore fluctuations. Do not try to out-guess the stock market. Buy a quality portfolio and invest for the long term."[13]

More recently Warren Buffett said simply, "I don't know how to tell what the market's going to do."[14]

Further, Peter Lynch said: "I spend about 15 minutes a year on economic analysis. The way you lose money in the stock market is to start off with an economic picture. I also spend 15 minutes a year on where the stock market is going."[15] American Funds, Washington Mutual Fund founder Bernie Nees was asked how to make money in the stock market. He answered, "You must be invested at the bottom." When asked how one can be guaranteed that they are at the bottom he said, "Always be invested."[16]

The best answer that I have ever heard to the question *Where is the market going?* was again from Peter Lynch: "Which way the next 1,000 to 2,000 points in the market will go is anybody's guess, but I believe strongly that the next 10,000, 20,000 and 40,000 points will be up."[17] He knew well that this was not a short-term prediction and that he may be describing a 10- or 20-year horizon, but he also knew that this is the only reasonable way to predict market returns.

That is a great answer. Remember that and never ask the question again. Why not? Because you cannot know the answer. It is never a good idea to ponder what you cannot know, unless you are in a philosophy class. Managing risk is not about guessing and predicting. Managing risk is about acting based on information that we do know, and not about acting on information that we cannot know. Or, as the Vanguard Group asks in one of their advertisements, *Why try to predict the market when it can't be predicted?* That is a sensible question. Take note of the fact that Vanguard is one of the world's largest money managers, and they are admitting that not only can we not predict the market, but neither can they. So, what they are saying is that you should invest but give up on this idea of trying to figure out where the Dow Jones

Industrial Average will be three years from now. And over $3 trillion worth of Vanguard managed assets seems to agree.

No, Really, I Mean It: Where's the Market Going?

The stock market as we know it in this country has been around since May 26, 1896. Between 1897 and 2014, it had a positive total return in 78 years and negative total return in 40 years. That is to say that the stock market has been up 66% of the time. But, it does not move quite so systematically. As Daniel Webster said, "Miracles do not cluster." Nor do market returns cluster.

The trouble is with the news media's minute-by-minute description of the stock market as either soaring or collapsing; with hyperventilating (and, of course, seductive) 20-year-old reporters yelling from the stock exchange floor as though they were on the sidelines of an NFL game; and with 3D color stock market updates on everyone's computer and television. The closer we are, the more spectacular is the view. This is the intent, so we don't take our eyes off the screen for the coming commercial.

Professional investors do not predict the market in the short term but they do in the long term. I have always thought that predicting the stock market is opposite of predicting the weather. As Gregg Ireland, portfolio counselor with the American Funds Group said, "Speculating what the stock market will do in the short term is like predicting the weather next week. It's an unpredictable variable."[18]

I do believe that there is, though, an interesting association between weather forecasting and stock market predicting. A meteorologist can tell within a degree or two what the high and low temperature will be tomorrow but has not a clue what the high and low will be tomorrow 10 years from now. Stock forecasting is the opposite: Analysts cannot tell you what the Dow Jones Industrial Average is going to do tomorrow but can tell you plus or minus a percentage point what the average annual return will be over the next 40 years. The longer the term, the more accurate the forecast. Think about that. This is the primary reason why the investment industry thinks long term and tries to get investors to think long term as well; their models get more accurate as the term lengthens. I think there is some integrity to that.

Crestmont Research president Ed Easterling would likely agree with this long-term approach. He wrote: "The stock market is not consistently predictable over months, quarters, or periods of a few years. The stock market is, however, quite predictable over periods approaching a decade or longer...."[19] And Bill Spitz, former manager of the Vanderbilt University endowment fund, said jokingly, "Avoid financial forecasting, but if you must, give either numbers or dates, but not both."[20]

Finally, to this point let's compare two professions: doctors and stock brokers. Doctors make predictions about how drugs will perform inside the human body—a closed system. Brokers make predictions about where prices will go in an open system—significantly more variables and little experiential returns data. One is possible; the other is not.

Even Short-Term Predictions Are Tough

Be careful with short-term predictions, too, or it will be terribly difficult to manage your money. For example, the Nikkei 225 (the Japanese equivalent to the Dow Jones Industrial Average) returned 24.30% annually for the five-year period from 1985 to 1989. A $10,000 investment would have tripled to $29,672. Those were transformative times. The Nikkei was booming and the Japanese were buying everything from golf courses in Hawaii to Rockefeller Center. America ate sushi for the first time, the first Japanese luxury car (called Lexus) was introduced, and virtually everyone was scared and excited about the ominous glow from the land of the rising sun. I, too, was entranced after reading William Gibson's hit novel, *Neuromancer,* about a futuristic make believe world in Chiba City, Japan, where man and machine were one.

Next, after this spectacular five-year market performance, from 1990 to 1994 the Nikkei 225 was down 49.3%. For the next 15 years the Nikkei would drop by another 50%. If you had doubled-down on Japan after 1989 you would have been very disappointed.

So, am I bullish or bearish? Neither. My favorite market strategist, Fritz Meyer, put it to me very succinctly: "The point is that you stay fully invested in a globally diversified portfolio and periodically re-balance—period. Being bullish or bearish has nothing to do with proper asset allocation and long-term investing. Trying to figure out whether you should be bullish or bearish at any given point implies you're trying to time the market in some fashion."[21]

Betting on the Past

When I first got into the investment business, I made the same rookie errors that all brokers make. One of the dumbest is to assemble yesterday's star performers into a buy list for your clients. Because I have always been good with numbers I was one of the original data miners and was the only broker in our large metropolitan Merrill Lynch office to bring in a computer every day to work. Boy, was I good at predicting the past! My list of favorites was always last year's top performers. This is like picking next year's Oscar winner from last year's list. In 86 years of Academy Awards only Spencer Tracy and Tom Hanks have ever won consecutive Best Actor awards. That's probably a better record than picking top performers for stocks or mutual funds.

Morningstar, Inc., the mutual fund research firm, created the star rating system that rates funds from one to five stars. Most mutual fund managers are obsessed with star ratings and are never shy about pounding their chests when they earn the coveted five stars, the highest ranking for risk-adjusted return. Here is why. "Studies show that more than 90% of all money flowing into funds goes into issues that carry four- or five-star ratings."[22] There is only one problem: Success is fleeting. Yesterday's five-star fund is likely not tomorrow's five-star fund. And yesterday's two-star fund may well be tomorrow's five-star fund. Recent studies by one of my favorite fund managers, the American Funds Group, and the Frank Russell Company bears this out. Figure 4-4 and Figure 4-5 show two consecutive eight-year periods that show the same thing. Top performance is apparently impossible to maintain in the investment world. Notice where the first quartile money managers tend to end up four years later, and where the first-quartile money managers come from. The best get worse, and the worse get better.

How Many Stars Was That Fund Again?[23]

Historical performance does not predict future returns.

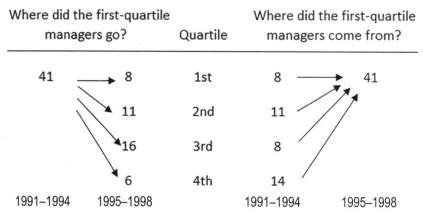

Where did the first-quartile managers go?		Quartile	Where did the first-quartile managers come from?	
41	8	1st	8	41
	11	2nd	11	
	16	3rd	8	
	6	4th	14	
1991–1994	1995–1998		1991–1994	1995–1998

Universe consists of 162 institutional managers in Russell's growth, market-oriented, and value universes with eight years of history through December 31, 1998.

Figure 4-4

How Many Stars Was That Fund Again?[24]

Historical performance does not predict future returns.

Where did the first-quartile managers go?		Quartile	Where did the first-quartile managers come from?	
55	21	1st	21	55
	11	2nd	12	
	9	3rd	12	
	14	4th	2	
1998–2001	2002–2005		1998–2001	2002–2005

Universe consists of 200 institutional managers in Russell's growth, market-oriented, and value universes with eight years of history through December 31, 2005.

Figure 4-5

The numbers were recently brought up to date. Figure 4-6 illustrates the same conclusion:

How Many Stars Was That Fund Again?[25]

Historical performance does not predict future returns.

Where did the first-quartile managers go?		Quartile	Where did the first-quartile managers come from?	
Top Quartile	14%	1st	12%	Top Quartile
	18%	2nd	9%	
	16%	3rd	8%	
	30%	4th	29%	
	22%[1]		41%[2]	
5 Years	5 Years		5 Years	5 Years
2004–2008	2009–2013		2004–2008	2009–2013

Universe consists of 3,964 U.S. equity large cap blend managers.
1) 22% of top quartile managers from 2004 to 2008 are no longer included within the Morningstar U.S. large blend category.
2) 41% of top quartile managers from 2009 to 2013 did not have a five-year track record during the previous period.

Figure 4-6

Corroborating evidence came from another authoritative research firm that concluded: "Nearly half of the value managers that earned a first-quartile rank for three-year performance in 2005 did so again in 2007. Between 2007 and 2009, only one-fourth managed to hold their top-quartile berth."[26]

Another study showed that "performance typically fails to persist in the future."[27] Aye Soe and Frank Luo reviewed 1,020 domestic actively managed mutual funds and found "[f]or the five years ending March 2012, only about 5 percent of the funds maintained top-half performance rankings over five consecutive 12-month periods...."[28]

E vidence of Investor Fails

None of us would crowd into Walmart after it announces it has increased its prices on all of its products, and then flee after it slashed prices. However, this is exactly how retail investors tend to behave. What they are showing when they do this is that they are predicting the stock market. Very simply, they are saying that the market just dropped, so it will continue to go down, or the market just went up so it will continue to rise. There are many examples of this. The latest example is illustrated in Figure 4-7 on page 135, in which I have combined the returns of the S&P 500 from 2008 through 2013 with a Gallup poll that shows stock ownership. Despite the stock market reaching record highs in 2013, Gallup discovered that stock ownership was at its lowest level since 1998, the year it began recording its poll.[29]

There is something missing in this relationship between the stock market and the investor. I believe the missing piece is the advisor. The advisor is the dispassionate third party who is aware of long-term market trends and can keep you in the stock market even when it drops. Yes, the stock market dropped 37% in 2008. But in four years, had you held on, your portfolio would have fully recovered. And after the next year you would have been rewarded with an additional 32% return. This is why advisors tend to say "think long term" and "buy and hold." This is hard to do when you are advising yourself, as we are all naturally ruled by our emotions.

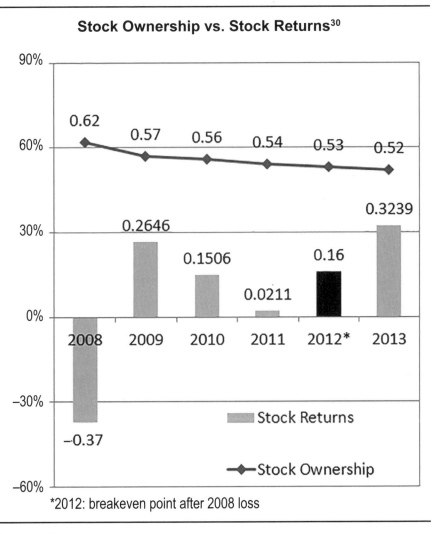

Figure 4-7

Investors tend to underperform the very markets that they are investing in. The data from multiple sources that I have included have already spoken to that. Additionally, this data from ETF.com[31] shows how unlikely top performing funds will remain in their respective high positions for the next four years. (See Figure 4-8.) Almost all of the top performers lost their lofty rankings. Fund performance is much like the career of the average NFL running back that lasts roughly five years and has one peak year of the five.

Top Funds Poor Performance in Consecutive 12-Month Periods[32]

Mutual Fund Category	Fund Count	% Remaining in Top Quartile			
	2007	2008	2009	2010	2011
All Domestic Funds	513	13.1	5.5	0.4	0.0
Large-Cap Funds	157	10.8	6.4	0.0	0.0
Mid-Cap Funds	88	13.6	3.4	0.0	0.0
Small-Cap Funds	116	19.8	8.6	0.9	0.0
Multi-Cap Funds	152	9.9	3.3	0.7	0.0

Mutual Fund Category	Fund Count	% Remaining in Top Half			
	2007	2008	2009	2010	2011
All Domestic Funds	1025	35.8	20.3	5.2	1.6
Large-Cap Funds	313	28.8	16.3	4.2	1.0
Small-Cap Funds	232	49.1	31.9	10.3	2.6
Multi-Cap Funds	304	33.6	16.1	3.6	1.6

Figure 4-8

However, why should I blame you (the investor) and not the fund manager for this? After all, you have no control over the fund manager and his or her performance. The reason why I am focused on you, the investor, is precisely because you have no control over fund performance. Despite this fact, investors tend to chase returns. Michael Rawson, CFA, with Morningstar, Inc. recently released data that showed that investors overwhelmingly favor past performance with their investment dollars. In 2013 investors put $228 billion into Morningstar four- and five-star funds and withdrew $192 billion in one-, two-, and three-star funds.[33]

Investors are making a classic blunder by investing in past performance. A better approach would be to match up asset classes with your risk tolerance and investment objectives, irrespective of past performance of funds. But, we are only in the analysis stage now. In the final chapter we will talk about more effective ways, in my opinion, to choose investments.

So, What *Can* You Predict? (A Negative Example)

Quit predicting the stock market or manager performance. There is only one financial asset that you need to predict: your savings. Frankly, it is more important to ask the right questions than it is to know the right answers. Therefore, it is more important to ask where you are going instead of where the market is going. That question (*Where am I going?*) is always on the mind of my wealthier clients. They are internally focused, not externally focused. I believe this has to do with ego and self-preservation: They just think about themselves more than the average person—a blessing and a curse.

Let this survey illustrate my point about focusing on you before we move further. This survey was conducted more than 10 years ago, per a survey of investors, and it was promulgated by AIM Funds (now Invesco). You may have to read the questions and answers two or three times to believe it. Here are the three questions and the most frequent answers.

Retirement Study: A True Story

1) Do you think you'll have enough money in retirement?

   Yes ✓   No

2) Do you know how much you will need?

   Yes   No ✓

3) Have you actually started saving for retirement?

   Yes   No ✓

To review, the average person has not started saving for retirement, nor does he know how much he will need. What he does know is that he will have enough money. If you were looking for a definition of virtual reality, I think this is it. This might be why there are 338,000 results when you Google "investment books" and 5,110,000 results when you search for "Jell-O." Those of us in the investment business have job security as long as these facts remain.

The 4 Types of Investors

I believe that closing the gap between virtual reality and reality can be urged along by evaluating what type of investor you are. Expectations can be much easier managed if the investor has a better sense of his or her personal investment characteristics. I ask prospective clients the following two questions: *If the stock market was up 12% in a given year, what would you expect the return on your portfolio to be? If the stock market was down 12% in a given year, what would you expect the loss on your portfolio to be?* The questions are general enough to get them thinking.

The answers are often surprising. First, a disclaimer: *There is a right answer.* Yes, you read that correctly, I did not say that there is no right answer. There is no right answer in the fields of comparative literature, or Eastern spirituality, or modern art, but in the investment world there are right answers and wrong answers. Right answers bring you greater risk-adjusted returns over the long term; wrong answers bring you lesser risk-adjusted returns over the long term. I will give you the two right answers and the two wrong answers to the questions.

There are four possible responses to each question: You expect your portfolio return to be greater than 12% (>), or lesser than 12% (<) in an up market, and you expect your portfolio return to be greater than –12% (>), or lesser than –12% (<) in a down market. (I could have picked 10, 11, or 13%. There's nothing fixed about the 12% number, but I wanted it to be slightly higher than average returns to stimulate thinking.)

The four types of investors:

1. Spectulator.
2. Dreamer.
3. Amateur.
4. Contrarian.

1. Speculator

Q: *If the stock market was up 12% in a given year, what would you expect the return on your portfolio to be?*

A: > 12%

Q: *If the stock market was down 12% in a given year, what would you expect the loss on your portfolio to be?*

A: < –12%

This is not an unrealistic response. Speculators expect greater returns when the market goes up and greater losses when the market drops. Professional speculators, venture capital, and private equity might fit this category. However, the way that a professional speculator makes money is by having a strict sell discipline in a down market (or by being in so many deals that the rare supernova investment eclipses the numerous asteroids). A strict sell discipline is what separates the professional from the accidental.

I don't think that the non-professional investor has the time, tools, or skills to monitor the risk of his portfolio to be an effective speculator. Note that I said *effective speculator.* We all know the ineffective speculators who simply want to beat an up market but are completely uninformed about down markets: day traders, IPO buyers, penny stock buyers, and so forth. Maybe you have known this person. Maybe you were this person.

Paul Tudor Jones is one of the great speculators of our time. Jones is primarily a commodities investor originally from Memphis, Tennessee. I met him in Atlanta years ago near the beginning of his career when he created a futures fund for Merrill Lynch. In 1987 he reportedly made between $80 and $100 million—more than anyone else on Wall Street. He currently has a net worth more than $4 billion. What philosophy guides him? "I'd say that my investment philosophy is that I don't take a lot of risk...at the end of the day, the most important thing is how good are you at risk control. Ninety percent of any great trader is going to be the risk control."[34]

2. Dreamer

Q: *If the stock market was up 12% in a given year, what would you expect the return on your portfolio to be?*

A: > 12%

Q: *If the stock market was down 12% in a given year, what would you expect the loss on your portfolio to be?*

A: > –12%

This answer is illogical and is the most dangerous investment philosophy to hold. Investment strategies that short-term outperform the market on the upside tend to be aggressive in nature, or employ leveraging techniques such as buying on margin or investing in options. Such strategies have the opposite effect in a down market and multiply losses. Now, a clever money manager might say that he employs aggressive strategies in up markets and conservative strategies in down markets, and that is how he plans on achieving superior returns in either market.

The problem is that we never know in advance whether we are in a good market or a bad market. A recent market debacle befell sub-prime bond investors; they didn't know that they were in a bad market until a few days before they folded their business and took multi-billion-dollar write-downs. A glaring example: "On Oct. 1 the bank disclosed that it was writing down $3.4 billion in losses largely due to ill-considered bets on the U.S. subprime market.... UBS held $19 billion in subprime residential mortgage-backed securities—90% or more of it rated AAA."[35] UBS, obviously, did not know what kind of a market it was in.

The investor who expects to outperform in an up market *and* a down market will be disappointed and eventually divest. Even professional money managers who would describe themselves as aggressive would not expect these kinds of returns nor promise them. Of all of the four choices, this is the one the investor should be highly suspicious of if his or her investment advisor promised such results.

3. Amateur

Q: *If the stock market was up 12% in a given year, what would you expect the return on your portfolio to be?*

A: < 12%

Q: *If the stock market was down 12% in a given year, what would you expect the loss on your portfolio to be?*

A: < –12%

This investor expects lower than market averages in good years and greater losses in bad years. Most studies would indicate that this is, in fact, what average investors return. They don't capture all of the upside but they lose more than the market in bad years. This was witnessed in the internet bubble and in any period of market excess when investors get into the market too late, thus never receiving any long-term benefit and exiting only after significant (*I'm never going to do that again*) losses. This is a wrong answer. If you really feel this way, you might be acting out of fear. If your fear is this great, you may not be suitable to be a stock investor.

4. Contrarian

Q: *If the stock market was up 12% in a given year, what would you expect the return on your portfolio to be?*

A: < 12%

Q: *If the stock market was down 12% in a given year, what would you expect the losses on your portfolio to be?*

A: > –12%

I believe this is the best answer for the non-professional long-term investor, and the most realistic route to positive returns. This investor realizes that the key to long-term wealth accumulation in the stock market is protection in down markets; thus he gives up some on the upside but protects on the downside.

Hedge-fund managers, whom many consider to be the savviest of professional money managers, would fit in this category. Brian Portnoy, PhD, CFA, wrote, "[M]ost hedge fund managers use hedging techniques, many of them will underperform in up markets and outperform in down markets. This speaks to a lower risk profile, not higher."[36]

Why does this work? Math. The numbers always work against you, and because they do, if your expectations and portfolio models this you are likelier to win. How do the numbers work against you? Call it investment gravity. Remember: If you lose 50% in one year how much do you need to make in the next year to break even? One hundred percent—twice as much. You need to absorb that and see how you can have investment gravity work for you. That is, realize that if you can only protect yourself during the down markets, your total return will be higher than the person who did not protect himself.

■　■　■

There actually is a fifth answer to the question: Whether the market goes up or down 12% you expect your returns to be neither greater than the market nor less than the market. You simply expect whatever the market returns. This answer would come from the committed index fund investor, and certainly a legitimate way to invest, as more than $2 trillion in exchange traded funds (ETF) and index funds attests.

Sorry, Your Expectations Don't Matter

Despite what kind of investor you are, contrarian, speculator, or indexer, in a sense your investment expectations are *not* important. By way of analogy, imagine that you are a physician. One of your patients who is terminal but has survived his third year of lung cancer says, "Doc, I want to live forever. Please help me." What would you do? Would you abandon all of your other patients for this one? Would you search through the *Journal of the American Medical Association* for a miracle cure? Would you go home and tell your spouse that you are taking a cot down to the lab and will not be home until you have found the magic elixir for curing this patient? Would you consult with your old medical school professors to see if there was some class in immortality that perhaps you missed? No. Unfortunately your patient's expectations are unrealistic. It is time for this patient to modify his objectives. Quality of remaining life, comfort, settling estate issues, and spiritual deliverance are more realistic.

The message for the doctor, patient, investment advisor, and you the investor is this: Expectations do not determine your objectives. Instead, your objectives drive your expectations. This is what I mean when I say to predict yourself, not the market. Example: When I meet with an older client who has significant financial assets, has plenty of income to live on, and does not need to grow those assets, what kind of investor is this? My first guess is conservative, not aggressive. I think some might say, *She has plenty of money and can afford to take risks.* My feeling is different. I would say, *She has plenty of income and does not need to grow her portfolio according to her, so why take a risk?* This is how objectives form expectations—but I could be wrong. Because I cannot predict the market, but can only predict you, based on what you have told me, I will track your objectives and build a portfolio accordingly.

The key is you, not the markets. That's why an advisor's first duty is to ask you scores of questions—to understand you. If your potential advisor has not asked you multiple questions, that should be a warning that you may have the wrong person.

Predict You, Not the Future

We spend too much time trying to predict the wrong thing (the market) instead of the most important thing (you).

There is even an equation for predicting the market called the *expected return* formula. It says that the expected return of an investment is a sum of the returns of all the investments:

$$E(R) = w_1 R_1 + w_2 R_2 + ... + w_n R_n$$

$E(R)$ is expected return, w equals weight (or % you have in this investment), and R is the return of the investment you are calculating (stocks, bonds, commodities, etc.). It is simply a weighted average formula. And, here's the good part: For it to work you have to predict what the returns will be for stocks, bonds, commodities, or whatever investment you are considering. Because the returns are unknown, adding these unknowns together only compounds the error.

Granted, if I had the choice, I would rather have the ability to consistently predict the future than the alternative. What is the alternative? Accepting that I cannot predict the future but investing anyway.

Don't give up. The question *Should I buy stocks or bonds?* is a good one. Nevertheless, it reminds me of an old insurance agent (who was previously a pro baseball player) in Florida who was with Penn Mutual Life when I was the regional sales manager for the broker/dealer in the early 1990s. I used to call him and try to get him to do more stock business with us instead of just selling insurance and fixed annuities.

I would show him impressive and colorful "mountain charts" that started with a $10,000 investment in 1929 growing to some huge number like $50,000,000 (I made that up) over a 60-year period. He told me once, "Thanks, Andy. I got your chart. Very persuasive. What nobody tells you is that back in 1929 nobody had $10,000."

Instead of impressive mountain charts, mountains that few investors ever actually climbed, ponder the chart in Figure 4-9. It shows the reality about us. The reality is that we are emotional creatures. Note that as stock market returns increased, investors' willingness to take risk increased. Divide the 22-year periods into three seven-year periods. Notice that in the first seven-year period (1988–1995) the measures of "willingness to take risks" (there are two similar measures from different sources represented by boxes and diamonds) were half as prevalent as for the next two seven-year periods. However, when was it a better time to invest: when the market was lower and flatter (first seven years), or when it is higher and more volatile (second and third seven-year periods)? We tend to be more interested in investing when the market is high.

This is the folly of being led by your expectations (*I think the market is going higher.*) rather than your objectives (*How much do I need to retire?*). Those who predict themselves rather than the market determine what direction they need to go, gather the resources, and implement their plan. Those who predict the market rather than themselves are constantly in and out of the market with no long-term plan or commitment.

Acceptance of Risk Tends to Move With the S&P 500[37]

Percentage of U.S. Households Willing to Take Above-Average Investment Risk, 1988–2010

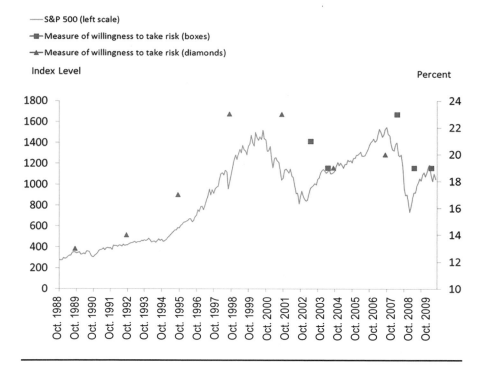

Figure 4-9

Ultimately their entire financial livelihood is tied to how they feel, instead of what they need.

Maybe this will help you understand what I am trying to say. Do you remember the movie *Caddyshack*? The clubby Ty Webb (Chevy Chase) instructs his caddy Danny Noonan (Michael O'Keefe) how to master the game of golf.

Danny. I'm going to give you a little advice. There's a force in the universe...that makes things happen. All you have to do is get in touch with it. Stop thinking. Let things happen...and be...the ball.

In a sense, I am saying *Be the investment.* Focus on you and your objectives, and not the markets, investments, or the complex language around the world of investing.

EXECUTE

~

Investments Don't Make Money—People Do:

Hiring an Advisor Is the Best Investment Plan You Can Make

> Only the gauche, the
> illiterate, the frightened and
> the pastless destroy money.
> —William Faulkner

I can tell you from 30 years of experience that the difference between successful investors and unsuccessful investors is the *investor,* not the *investment.*

With the advent of discount and robo-brokers, no-load mutual funds and exchange traded funds that cover all of the major investable asset classes are now widely available to anyone. Since the 1970s and the collapse of fixed commissions in the United States, we truly have witnessed a democratization of investing. All the investments are there and are available to everyone with no barriers to entry, and they are practically free. So, we should all be rich, right? Unfortunately, the only true barrier to successful investing that remains is the investor.

Help!

Ludwig Börne, the German writer known for saying "Nothing is permanent but change," also said, "Getting rid of a delusion makes us wiser than getting hold of a truth." Let's look at some possible delusions about what we can and cannot do for ourselves. Before stepping back into the investment world I usually prefer stories from real life. These are about three airline passenger emergencies and how they were handled.

A 747 passenger named Paula Dixon, from Aberdeen, Scotland, suffered a collapsed lung on a 14-hour flight from Hong Kong to London. Death was certain except for the lucky fact that two doctors on-board were able to save her using a coat hanger, a surgical tube, and some brandy as a disinfectant. One doctor remarked, "It was a little unpleasant when we went through the chest wall."[1] Dixon lived to laugh at that comment.

In another incident, a woman on an airplane suddenly stopped breathing. Again, on-board were two physicians. With a ball-point pen, a soda can, and some water, they were able to perform a tracheotomy on her and save her life.

Contrast those happy endings with a recent airline tragedy where a 46-year-old Haitian died while in flight from Port au Prince to New York on an Airbus A300-600. The flight had all the modern medical equipment that is required, including defibrillator and first aid oxygen. But, as the *Wall Street Journal* affirmed, "The decision on what action to take, especially in the early moments of a crisis, usually falls on the flight attendants."[2]

These life-and-death stories made me ask: *Would I rather have a full surgical facility on my next flight and two flight attendants to operate it (as in the last example), or nothing on-board but stale peanuts and sodas, and two physicians sitting next to me?* It was clear from reading these stories that it was the expertise and ingenuity of the physicians that saved the passengers' lives, not the equipment—unless you want to call a soda can and a ball-point pen emergency medical equipment.

What does this have to do with successful investing? If we are to believe the investment advice from the popular press, all you need to be successful as an investor is a no-load index fund and an internet connection—the equivalent of medical equipment and a flight attendant. But ask these questions: *What if the market suddenly drops 1,000 points? What if you lose your job and have to make some hard decisions about your money? What if you need to get a higher return in your IRA but really don't know the difference among a stock, an ETF, a mutual fund, and a limited partnership? Or, what if you need to save for your child's education but don't know the difference among a 529 Plan, UGMA, Coverdell ESA, annuity, or savings bond? Or worse, what if you are simply scared or don't know what to do?* Again, the difference is people (the physician or advisor), not the equipment (defibrillator or no-load fund).

First, What Doesn't Work?

I want you to hire an advisor, but I don't want you to hire just any advisor. And I want you to invest, but you must be smart about it. Maybe this story will help. I used to live in Manhattan and work for Merrill Lynch. I picked out a territory between 8th and 14th streets on the east and west sides of Fifth Avenue to prospect—basically the East Village. I discovered in the *Cole Criss-Cross* phone directory that the residents of that area were wealthy, were college educated, and had few children. I liked the "had few children" part because I figured my future clients wouldn't be wasting their potential investment money on birthday cakes, braces, bicycles, Brownie uniforms, and Big Wheels. It was a good combination for potential discretionary assets to help launch my investment career.

I pounded the list and became a cold-calling cowboy. Mostly I sold New York municipal bonds to widows. I liked them. They were fun and smart, not particularly rich (it took me a couple years to realize that the money was on the Upper East Side), but good for 10 or 20 bonds, and a good joke, every time I called.

They weren't all widows. One was a brilliant polio survivor named Flatow who worked for a major drug company. He sort of brought me up in the business. When I would get overexcited about a bond he would bellow, *Sheath thy happy dagger, boy.* Thus was my introduction to Shakespeare. Whenever I asked him for recommendations on how I might improve he'd say, *Sure. Why don't you take a long walk on a short pier?* Or, when I would launch into some long-winded explanation of a too-complex investment he would answer with *Allow me to misunderstand you.*

In one of my cold-calling marathons (I would often make 100 contacts a day, or until my ear hurt so much I couldn't hold the phone to it) I discovered another interesting chap named Joel, in Flatow's neighborhood. He was a musician, artist, and...options trader. He told me that he traded XMI, the *Major Market Index*. The Major Market Index is like the Dow Jones Industrial Average but with 20 stocks instead of 30. He and his business partner, John, had won the *Investor's Business Daily* options contest and were interested in telling me about their business as a way to get referrals from me.

I took the #6 train to Union Square from 59th Street to visit them. We met in a large sun-drenched room, the only furniture in which was a grand piano, which Joel played with great skill. They were charming and intelligent. Joel told me that he had a system. This is how most sophisticated investment conversations start. He could tell daily how the market would close as measured by the XMI. He said that he'd call me each morning to tell me if the market was going to close up or down. If I liked what I heard perhaps I would invest with him. It was like Doyle Lonnegan being set up by Kelly Hooker and Kid Twist, but I hadn't seen the movie *The Sting* yet, so I stayed in the game. Joel called for a month, which included about 20 trading days. He was never wrong. I couldn't believe it. Every day he told me the market would rise or fall, it did just that. I thought it was magic.

By the time Joel asked me if I wanted to introduce him to clients I was throwing names at him. I wanted all of my clients in this, but, no matter how fabulous this strategy was, I was still just 25 and could only get one client to give Joel

$10,000. You know the rest of the story. Joel stole it. Joel lost it. Joel got another $1,000,000 out of him and lost that. Actually, it was none of the above. After about a year there was somewhere around $5,000 in the account, so the client just closed the account, took his money, and went away.

I learned there really is no magical way to make money short term in the stock market. Even the number-one options trader in the country could not repeat his success long term.

Then, What Does Work?

Besides the folly of trading strategies that are short lived like the XMI options strategy, it's not a good idea to constantly fiddle with your portfolio by trying to pick the highs and the lows, or micromanaging your holdings. If you have carefully analyzed your portfolio selections based on your age, risk tolerance, financial objectives, investment experience, past track record, financial capabilities, family history, debt levels, and other factors, and have carefully created your asset allocation, then any other decision that you make with your portfolio should match those factors, and not just your notion that the market is too high, this stock is not performing as you expected, and so forth. In other words, don't make a change in three minutes when it took hours to build your portfolio.

Even after 30 years I am still surprised when a client calls me and says we need to make a change after the market drops 100 or 200 points. As if the hours of research, historical evaluations, calculations of risk tolerance and financial means and objectives did not already account for market drops. Think about it: You don't sell your house when it drops in value.

The best investors rarely look at their statements but could tell you plus or minus $5,000 what their multimillion-dollar net worth is, whereas the worst investors look at their accounts every day but couldn't tell you within $50,000 what their net worth is. Do you understand the difference? The best investors focus on what is important, like strategy, net worth, and income, but are insensitive to market fluctuations, bad or good news, or others' opinions.

Here are questions that you do not need to know specific answers to:

- What's the stock market going to do this year?
- Are interest rates going up or down?
- Who is going to win the election: a Democrat or a Republican?

Here are questions you do need specific answers to:

- What is my net worth (assets minus liabilities)?
- If my stock portfolio dropped by 20%, what would I do?
- How much time do I have to make this investment work?
- Am I a conservative, moderate, or aggressive investor?
- How much am I saving every month?

We can't go back to the lessons of Warren Buffett too many times. On a trip to a Berkshire Hathaway subsidiary factory in Dalian, China, Buffett was asked about his investment strategy. He said, "We don't go in and out of the markets. I simply look at individual businesses and try to figure out where they're likely to be in five or 10 or 20 years from now."[3] Likewise, think about yourself as a business.

Behave Yourself

When I think of Warren Buffett I think of the model of investor temperament. Investor (your) behavior is even more important than your investments. As Marshall Goldsmith, management consultant, said, "It's easy to know theories. It's hard to change behavior."[4] A wise investor will make more money on a lousy investment than an inexperienced investor will make on a superior investment. Want proof? There's lots of it. I've seen it in my practice. The clients who always second-guess me and their portfolio, buy and sell on a whim, and outsmart the market lose. Those who do the research, learn the fundamentals, like those presented in this book, and stick with their program usually win.

The wonderful author Pearl S. Buck wrote in *The Good Earth*, "Now five years is nothing in a man's life except when he is very young and very old." Investment programs are much like this. The most important times in an investment program are when you start and when you end. Your beliefs and behaviors, and how you manage yourself in the first five years sets the habits for the future. Wherever you are in life, think now that you are starting afresh.

Avoid These 8 Fatal Investing Errors

If you truly believe you can start fresh then it will pay to avoid what professors H. Kent Baker and Victor Ricciardi call "Common Behavioural Biases."[5] They have observed eight biases:[6]

1. **Representativeness,** or the fallacy of judging an investment good or bad because of past performance. The most recent example is gold and its collapse. I'll never forget all the investors I had to talk out of buying gold *after* it quadrupled in eight years to $1,700 per ounce.

2. **Regret,** or loss aversion. These investors avoid selling losers, even when they should, because it proves (they believe) that they made a bad decision.

3. **Disposition effect,** selling stocks whose prices have increased, while keeping stocks that are at a loss. Instead, consider cutting your losses and letting your profits run, as the pros do.

4. **Familiarity bias.** This is where investors buy what they know and avoid obscure investments. Commodities are a good example. Despite that commodities are a better inflation hedge than stocks, and are a good diversifier, they are universally avoided by average investors because commodities are unfamiliar.

5. **Worry.** Victor Ricciardi determined that 70% of investors associate stocks with the word "worry," whereas only 10% of investors associate bonds with worry. This is despite the fact that stocks have significantly outpaced bonds over the long term.

6. **Anchoring.** A great example of this is the financial meltdown from 2007 to 2009. Most investors were so anchored with the belief that the stock market is dangerous that they missed one of the most profitable recoveries in history.

7. **Self-attribution.** This is when an investor attributes a successful investment to his own talents, but assigns an uncontrollable force to negative outcomes. This is the bias that day-traders suffer from, leads to overconfidence, and the reason why most of them lose in the end.

8. **Trend chasing,** when investors chase last year's performance—this year. These are the ones who only buy Morningstar five-star funds. We saw in Day 4 how that strategy tends to work.

Eight no-gos are a lot to remember, I will admit, but they are important. A hint from Baker and Ricciardi: "[A]ppropriate financial planning policies can play a powerful role in keeping clients committed to a consistent and disciplined course of action and in avoiding such biases."[7] How can we successfully fight these biases?

Fire Yourself

I know, that sounds harsh, so I will soften it: Give yourself two weeks' notice.

The fact is we need help, particularly the more complicated and dangerous our lives become. I am not going to pretend that you can do this by yourself. As the British rock band Talk Talk lamented in a popular song: *Truth gets harder, there's no sense in lying / Help me find a way from this maze, I can't help myself.*[8] Sorry to say, this is not a self-help book. Surprised? Never have there been more self-help books available and more depressed people. For example, the number of patients diagnosed with depression increases by approximately 20% yearly. Meanwhile the market for self-improvement products and services is $9.8 billion with sales of self-improvement books expected to continue to grow significantly.[9]

There is no substitute for professional help when dealing with depression and other medical conditions, learning a new skill, or just about anything else you need help with.

The best example may be the daily battle with our belts. There are thousands of weight-loss books; their number seems to grow even faster than our weight. Yet, according to the National Health and Nutrition Examination Survey from the National Institutes of Health (NIH) more than two-thirds of Americans are overweight. The American Council on Exercise wrote, "While there is clearly no magic bullet to successfully losing weight, a new study suggests that health coaches may be the next best thing."[10] They refer to a study funded by the NIH and conducted by The Miriam Hospital's Weight Control and Diabetes Research Center in Providence, Rhode Island, which showed that overweight participants who worked with a professional health coach lost more weight than those who merely worked with a mentor or peer.[11]

There is no substitute for committed and accountable professional help. I believe that the simple pictures in Figure 5-1 and Figure 5-2 accurately illustrate the advantage of working with professionals over simply reading self-help books.

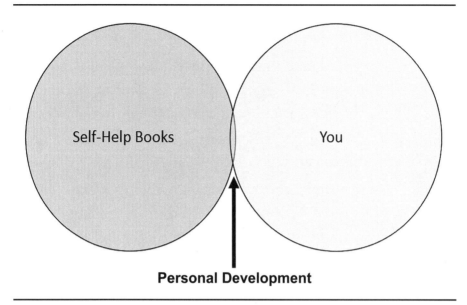

Figure 5.1

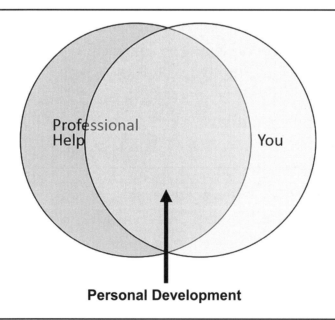

Figure 5.2

The message from the self-help industry is that you can do everything by yourself—thus "self-help." And of course, this is so you will buy more self-help books, tapes, seminars, programs, and so forth. I am not going to consign you to such a dismal and depressing fate in the multifarious and unforgiving investment world. I would rather be honest with you. You need attentive, personal, customized help from a financial advisor. If that is all you get out of this book, then I have accomplished my mission.

John MacDonald, first prime minister of Canada, said, "I need friends with me not when they think I'm right but when they think I'm wrong." Likewise, the power of an investment adviser is that he or she will help guide you during the tough periods to keep from selling when the market drops and buying too much at the peaks. That is to say that you should consider an adviser who has lived through many financial catastrophes yet stayed true to his or her strategy and performed well.

And regarding the complexity of investing there are now more ways to invest (number of mutual funds) than there are investments (number of stocks). Each way to invest (these new funds) is an attempt to answer the question *How should I invest?* Therefore let's ask the question: *How should I invest?*

Investing Like a Pro Means Hiring a Pro

We will hear again from James C. Bradford, Jr. Bradford (whom he preferred everyone call Jimmy) was a disarmingly pleasant and unpretentious man and the only Southerner who sat on the board of the NYSE. Perhaps as a reflection of his refinement he told me that he preferred the old term *customer's man* to *investment advisor* because it described better the personal relationship with the client: "He's working for you. People were to come to you on your reputation. Today it's a little more adversarial, as NPR says, go get a no-load fund, which is fine, but which no-load fund, or somebody to lead you through the thicket?"[12] Again, products are not the key, people are. Just as sick people need doctors, investors need advisors.

Could an advisor help you become wealthier? Writer Lewis Schiff catalogued the seven habits of the ultra-wealthy from his book *Business Brilliant.*[13] Schiff wrote: "Exceptional execution requires those who are business brilliant to focus on the two or three things they do very well. So they get their work done by building teams with complementary capabilities. Surveys show that most people, though, would rather learn to do tasks they're bad at than get others to do them." In Schiff's rankings, *"I hire people who are smarter than I am"* is number 4. In my rankings this would be number 1.

A professional's primary objective is to help his or her client do what they are bad at, but particularly to manage expectations. Good doctors do not dilute their prognoses; good lawyers do not misrepresent the strength of your case; accountants do not diminish the possibility of an audit; and good investment advisors do not overestimate the potential in your portfolio.

How Do I Start?

Be careful with your money. Evaluate the custodian you choose, the investment manager, the clearing firm, the individual securities or funds, the investment advisor, his or her CRD Status Report on FINRA's "Broker Check," and the advisor's employees.

Evaluate everyone—especially *you*.

Here is what I mean. Though I am not a risk-taker, I did skydive about 30 times years ago. Per *incident,* it is less risky than scuba diving—that is, diving in the air is less lethal than diving in the water. Remember: I am all about risk; I checked it out first. It is a thrilling sport. It is also quite complex. After you have been involved with it for a while you are expected to buy your own gear (parachute, jumpsuit, altimeter, goggles, helmet, etc.) and pack your own parachute. That's when I quit. I know me. I am just not very mechanical, and I knew that if I had to pack my own parachute I would forget important details, tie knots into lines that should be left untied, and leave untied lines that should be knotted. I knew that the sport was not safe in my hands, so I quit.

Well, not exactly. In truth, my brother, the owner of the drop zone, threw me out of the sport. Here's how it happened. One warm summer Saturday afternoon in Tullahoma, Tennessee, I jumped alone out of my brother's 1956 Cessna 182 at 10,000 feet. Side note: I have always been bad with directions. Not a problem when you are driving around in your car looking for PetSmart in a mall. Definitely a problem when you are falling in the sky at 120 miles per hour and have about three minutes to lock in a safe landing spot 2 miles below. Think of a skydiver as a bullet shot from a gun: Once the gun is aimed and fired the bullet has to continue in the same direction. Skydivers can make slight adjustments with steering toggles by turning left or right, but if you don't make path corrections at a higher altitude, your landing spot becomes less and less governable.

That's what happened to me. I sort of daydreamed (one of my dominant traits) for the first 7,000 feet downward, so at a certain point it was too late. I was headed for an active runway. (Hint: Runways are for airplanes; soft and forgiving grass is for skydivers.) As I was descending to the asphalt my problems compounded when an airplane taking off, which could not just stop in mid-air, powered right at me and just barely missed my parachute with its landing gear. The pilot looked right me, astonished, with his mouth wide open in the *Wha' the hell?* position.

I was floating at about 200 feet, was scared, and had never seen asphalt growing in my view through my goggles—only grass. It would otherwise not be a big deal to land on asphalt, but it is impossible to "land" when you hit the brakes (by yanking down both toggles simultaneously) at 20 feet—which is what I did. Usually you brake at about 6 feet. At 20 feet I stalled in the air and then free-fell fast at a 45-degree angle to the asphalt, and skidded on my hands and knees in a pathetic and embarrassing runway belly flop. I tore up my brother's jumpsuit, gloves, altimeter—oh, and my hands and knees.

As I gathered up the parachute and limped back to the drop zone, my brother looked at my bloody knees and hands and his torn-up jumpsuit, and said in disgust, *You need your own gear.* Then he grounded me.

I have also been interested in being a pilot over the years, an inborn trait in my family. But I also know that all of the prep work—equipment and fuel checks, navigation data, and aerodynamics—would be way beyond my temperament. So I leave the flying to Southwest Airlines.

Should You Do it Yourself?

Why do I mention this? Skydiving and flying are very dangerous if you are not really good at them—like the expression *There is no such thing as a pretty good alligator wrestler.* If you are no good at skydiving, flying, alligator wrestling, or investing, then, before you have a serious accident, stop doing it yourself.

However, when it comes to the details of accounting, data analysis, finance, economics, money management, asset allocation—the tools of investing—I feel at home. I have a few degrees, lots of licenses and experience, and read and write about investing, and I constantly study. Therefore, managing my clients' money, and my own money, is something that seems natural to me. The details are not overwhelming or scary.

You need to stop now and ask yourself: Are you more like Andy the skydiver, who can't be trifled by the details and is therefore the most dangerous flying object in the sky, or Andy the money manager, who is consumed and reasonably skilled? This is a very important question. You need to decide if fundamentally you *should* be managing your money by yourself, or if you need help.

I am not asking you if you feel lucky, or if you have had a few winners in the stock market. I am asking you if you know that you are competent in investment analysis, bookkeeping, organizing data, reading financial statements, and keeping up with tax law changes; are a student of financial instruments (know the difference, say, between a UIT, ETF, and CMO); and are comfortable with the math of compounding interest, internal rates of return calculations, percentages, probability and statistics, risk measurement, estate planning issues, and the like. If you are not, get out of the cockpit before you crash. Remember: It's not just you; your family is riding in the back.

When I hear the expression *do-it-yourself investor*, I think of *do-it-yourself parent* or *do-it-yourself doctor* or *do-it-yourself electrician*. The facts are sobering. Single parents are much likelier to be impoverished than two-parent households: "Among all children living only with their mother, nearly half—or 45%—live below the poverty line, the Census Bureau said.... By comparison, only about 13% of children with both parents present in the household live below the poverty line."[14] I don't wish to sound callous—sometimes single parenting is thrust upon us—but it should never be a choice.

Do I have to explain why do-it-yourself doctor or do-it-yourself electrician is not a good idea?

Something is not working. The fact is that the average net worth in the United States was $56,000 in 2013.[15] Try to retire on that. Face it: We need help.

Trust: The Most Important Trait

If you agree to leave the flying to someone more experienced, let's examine how to choose an advisor and what traits are essential.

First: how *not* to choose an advisor. I am religious but have always been suspicious of "faith-based" investing. Why? For the same reason that I am suspicious of "socially responsible" investing, and for the same reason that I am suspicious of "affinity" investing—or, in the case of Bernie Madoff, "affinity fraud." According to the SEC, affinity fraud "refers to investment scams that prey upon members of identifiable groups, such as religious or ethnic communities, the elderly or professional groups."[16] These appellations at times can be a decoy or just a manipulative marketing program. The proper way to evaluate an investment advisor, instead of *We worship in the same pews* (faith-based investing), or *I care more than they do* (socially responsible investing), or *We're members of the same country club* (affinity investing) is this: You need to evaluate your advisor or money manager in this order:

1. Trust.

2. Competence.

3. Fit.

If the advisor does not pass the *trust* test, then there is no need to check *competence*. If he or she does not pass the *competence* tests, then there is no need to check for *fit*. Faith-based, socially responsible, and affinity investing start with *fit* and rarely move backward through the more important steps. Why bother? You are already hooked. As an example, many otherwise-shrewd people invested with Bernie Madoff simply because he was Jewish (faith-based investing); others invested with him because he posed as an elite (affinity investing).

Heed the warning of William Cecil Burleigh: *Win hearts and you have all men's hands and purses.* Do not let a prospective advisor or money manager win your heart unless you have first determined if he or she is honest and capable. He or she should win your head first. Start with Finra.org's "Broker Check." You can view registered investment advisors, too.

Let's look closer at Madoff. I was startled by what I learned about Madoff's firm. "There was no independent custodian involved who could prove the existence of assets," said Chris Addy, founder of Montreal-based Castle Hall Alternatives, which reviews hedge funds for wealthy clients.[17] It is a vital question to know the custodian of your investment accounts and to be able to independently verify your balances. Additionally, Madoff kept the financial statement from the firm under lock and key and was "cryptic" about the firm's investment business.[18] Any reason, so far, to have trust issues with this advisor?

One out of four investors surveyed will write a check without having studied the financial statements of a fund. Nearly one in three will not always run a background check on fund manager. "Due diligence," says Stephen McMenamin of the

Greenwich Roundtable, "is the art of asking good questions."[19] It's also the art of not taking answers on faith.

After 30-plus years in the business, I have met a few con men. I can tell you that they are the nicest people you will ever encounter. You will feel an instant fit, and forgo the trust and competency review that I recommend. Remember that "con" is short for confidence. They steal your money only after they have stolen your confidence. It is interesting to hear investors talk about them after the scam. Always heard is *How could he do that to me? He was such a nice guy.* This is not the way the swindler thinks. I believe that most crooks in the investment industry do not mean to steal your money, but only to use it to enrich themselves, and then somehow, they will return your money. It rarely works out like that.

Don't think that sophisticated investors are immune to swindlers. They are not. The biggest investment theft that I ever was unfortunate to observe happened to the most sophisticated investors I knew.

What Is Competence?

If your prospective advisor passes the trust test, next is competence. Competence in an investment advisor is the hardest to measure of the three desired traits. The obvious achievements to look for are at least a bachelor's degree in economics, finance, accounting, math, or some other business discipline; appropriate securities licenses and/or recognized certifications such as CFP, CIMA, CFA, CHFC, CLU, or CPA; and at least three or four years of experience.

Warning: Many investment advisors spend time and money to look appealing (great office, fresh coffee always available, ready smile, pleasant assistants, etc.). You feel like you are with the concierge of a five-star hotel with this advisor. That's fine—but that is fit, not competency. Again, look for that last. I can't tell you how many people I know who selected an advisor with the following criteria: *He was nice, He had a great office,* and *My neighbor really likes him.* Remember: You're not looking for a buddy; you are looking for a very important trusted advisor.

Here are some questions you can ask that will quickly get to the competency level of your proposed advisor:

- What did the financial crisis of 2008 teach you?

- What is your personal expertise?

- What is the biggest loss any of your clients has taken?

- What general rate of return would you expect for the long-term moderate-risk-tolerance investor?

- What type of investors are not a good fit for your practice?

- What are the dollar ranges of your accounts— smallest to largest?

- What would be some ways for each of us to manage expectations?

- Which custodian(s) do you use?

- How can I contact them directly and view my account?

I am not going to propose specific answers for those questions. I'd rather you take a look at these and see what sorts of "interview" questions you should ask. Finally, don't listen to your friends' recommendations unless they assure you that they have checked the three criteria thoroughly.

F^{it}

As I have mentioned, *fit* is the least important of the three attributes for a suitable advisor for your financial future. But, it is important enough to be one of the three criteria in selecting an advisor. What is fit? Fit, in this case, is a merger of personal styles. If you are an objectives-based, hard-charging, goals-oriented executive, a slow-moving, generalist advisor would be a bad fit. If you value good listeners and all your advisor wants to do is talk over you, this is not a good fit. If you are a "people" person and your potential advisor asks no questions about you, then nothing will change in your professional relationship. Again—bad fit. However, think about your best friend for a minute. If your potential advisor seems like him or her, or has some of the same characteristics, you may be getting close. A good fit will make for a much more pleasurable and productive relationship.

■　▪　■

Trust, competency, and then fit. Additionally, you should use these attributes after the hire as well. If you are thinking about firing your advisor simply because lately he or she seems too busy or slightly less enthusiastic about you, stop and ask yourself if your advisor is still trustworthy and competent. Only if he or she fails in those two should you start shopping for a new advisor.

A re You Cargo, Passenger, or Co-Pilot?

We've discussed advisors. Now let's focus on you. Who are you? You should ask yourself. In all areas of life we should know our strengths and weaknesses. This is especially true when it comes to your money.

When it comes to investing, are you cargo, passenger, or co-pilot? Or, what investor personality type are you? Imagine an airplane. Cargo, like your suitcase, just needs to ride underneath in the storage area. Passengers, however, want to know where they are going, want to plan the trip, and enjoy looking out the window. Co-pilots are that and are also capable of actually flying the plane.

Which are you as an investor? Ask yourself honestly. I have all three types of clients. One is not better than the others. Cargo could not tell you the difference between a stock and a bond. But that doesn't mean they can't be excellent investors with the help of a patient advisor. Passengers are competent or at least curious investors, and want to learn more and follow a plan. Co-pilots are experienced able investors, are equipped to invest themselves, but still need help.

Now relate these three investor types back to *fit*. If your advisor treats you like cargo but you know you are a co-pilot we have a problem. Your objectives, and maybe your ego, will never be satisfied. If he treats you like a co-pilot but you are cargo, you are in for a scary ride. You don't want to hold the wheel for takeoffs and landings; you just want to get there. I was fired by an important client because I treated them like passengers. They really wanted to be more in control of their investments than I thought they did. I discovered too late that they were co-pilots. It was my fault. Lesson learned. Perhaps it will be easier having this type of "fit" discussion with your advisor if you frame it in these terms instead of trying to decide if your tastes in restaurants, movies, or politics are similar—which is unimportant.

Investors Often Do Better With Advisors

Here's some encouraging news about working with an advisor. Many studies indicate that investor returns can go up by working with an advisor. Of course there are no guarantees, but the studies are compelling. In a 2007 study conducted by Charles Schwab, participants in retirement plans who did not work with an advisor returned 11.1%, versus 14.1% return for those who worked with an advisor.

Another study evaluated 401(k) plan investors. The study reviewed 14 large retirement plans with more than 723,000 participants. It found that those using help (described as using a target date fund, a managed account, or online advice) now account for 34.4% of all 401(k) participants, up from 30% in 2011. The results? "Between 2006 and 2012, participants in 401(k) plans who paid extra for advice earned an average of 3.32 percentage points more per year, after fees, than those taking do-it-yourself approach. If continued over 20 years, that annual performance edge would boost retirement wealth by 79%," according to the report.[20]

After all, 82% of investors with over $150,000 seek advice from financial advisors. This is roughly 15 million house-holds.[21] And, the Investment Company Institute found that mutual fund holders with incomes of $100,000 or more are 10 times more likely to have an ongoing relationship with an advisor than those earning less than $35,000.[22] It is typically wealthier investors with complex lives who use investment advisers. Perhaps you are one of them, or wish to be.

Do you remember the statistics from Dalbar, Inc. that showed that investors typically underperform the markets? One very important job of an advisor is to keep investors in the markets even during choppy times so they get out of the habit of selling and thereby missing the superior long-term gains that can be earned from being a consistent investor.

The rough composite of the go-it-alone investor looks like this to me: He saw on CNN that no-load funds are better than load funds because they are "free." He also saw somewhere that stocks are good investments. To complete his education, a friend told him that indexes outperform active managers. So when he adds up the three things that he knows about invest-ing he puts all of his money into an S&P 500 no-load index fund and boasts about his investing prowess. Net result? In the 10-year period through December 31, 2008, he lost money. He gets mad, grumbles about "greed and corruption" on Wall Street, takes his money out of the market altogether, puts everything into a low-yielding money market fund, and retires on far less than he could have had. These are the *I used to invest in the stock market but lost money* kind of stories that I have heard for years. Rarely do these unfortunate people have advisors.

Retail investors spend most of their investment research time (which is overall less than two hours per year) evaluating funds' cost, past performance, brand recognition, and what their friends say about the investment; but not more important items like asset classes, management styles, or their own investment objectives. It is no surprise that they are the first to jump overboard when their fund hits a big wave.

Just as a doctor doesn't just throw drugs at you and disappear, financial advisors attempt to protect investors from the market. I believe that professional money managers are the best protection against market uncertainties, and best poised to take advantage of the market when it goes up. "Among U.S. investors, retirees and investors with $100,000 or more in invested assets are significantly more likely than their counterparts to use a dedicated financial adviser."[23] The same Gallup survey showed that "U.S. investors are more likely to have a dedicated financial adviser than to use a financial website for obtaining advice on investing or planning for their retirement, 44% vs. 20%."[24]

It's Not Just About Cost

Are advisors too expensive? Just as there are expensive five-star hotels and cheap one-star hotels, there is more to advisors than cost. It is the same with any profession. Lawyers are measured by their success in court and relieving clients' anxieties. When you hire a contractor to lay a wood floor, you don't complain when hardwood is more expensive than laminate. So why is it that critics pay so much attention to costs and not the effectiveness of the advisor? I cannot guarantee the performance of any fund, but I am reasonably sure that a superior advisor will add value.

Jason Zweig, whom I mentioned previously, wrote: "Of course, much of the value of a financial adviser can't be captured by measuring the track record of his investment picks alone. By reducing your taxes, planning your estate and retirement, cutting your debt and adjusting your insurance coverage, an adviser can make you much richer and more secure."[25] Perhaps this is why direct sales of mutual funds have dropped in half since 1990 (ICI). Investors seek guidance now more than ever from financial advisors.

Why Else Should I Hire an Investment Advisor?

Because an advisor will do just about anything for you: keep records, fill out forms, provide second opinions, administer your accounts, income plan, compare complex investments, help with tax and estate issues, protect you from bad ideas, and generally watch over you.

Here are some examples from my own practice over the years. Most of these tasks were done for free and are simply incidental tasks that most advisors perform:

◻ Helped client retrieve cash value from complex insurance policy that was unsuitable. This may have saved client more than $100,000.

- Helped client retrieve $75,000 in state reclaimed bonds from a major bank. This took hours of work.

- Kept client from dealing with a fraudulent mortgage broker who likely would have absconded with the proceeds of a refinance cash-out. Also alerted the FBI.

- Notified and corrected a major insurance company that went seven years without properly informing an elderly client that she had required minimum distributions due from her IRA, possibly saving her from tax consequences.

- Provided records for a client going through a divorce, which proved his premarital assets. This saved thousands of dollars in his settlement.

- Encouraged client to keep an annuity with only $800 cash value to protect a $10,000 death benefit, which later paid to estate.

- Put client into a variable annuity in 1993. Then moved to a fixed annuity in December 2001, at peak of stock market and interest rates, thereby locking in gains and providing high income.

- Kept eager client out of stocks in the tech bubble of 1999, saving thousands of dollars. He later sent me a thank-you note.

- Invested client into a variable annuity. Client died in 2004 and death benefit of $10,900 paid out to widow while cash value was only $5,500.

- Joined client at local Social Security office to help him wade through the complex regulations in preparation for his retirement.

- Advised client who was going through marital problems to keep his inheritance separate from his wife. They later divorced and he lost far less money than he would have.

- Made multiple clients and prospects aware of the opportunities within their mutual funds to reduce commissions through break-point pricing; and actively search clients' accounts outside of my firm to reduce commissions.

- Discovered client could rebuy his mutual fund he had earlier sold at net asset value (no commission). He was not aware of this.

- Advised client to use appreciated stock instead of cash to make a charitable contribution for $10,000 to save taxes and commission. Tax savings was $520. Then advised him to wait until after the ex-dividend date to transfer to pick up $100 dividend.

- Discovered 13 of 23 U.S. savings bonds for client had already come due and were no longer paying interest. She cashed in to reinvest.

- Advised client who had quit smoking three years before to call his insurance company to re-rate his policy to non-smoker to save him money.

- Advised client to wait a day to sell stock to pick up the quarterly dividend of $969. This has happened many times with clients.

◻ Expedited annuity application paperwork (at my expense), which earned client 8½% rather than 8% on his fixed DCA (dollar cost averaging) account.

◻ Saved client $21,000 from a predatory company that improperly attempted to escheat (transfer to the state) 1,544 book-entry Chevron shares of stock. I needed the help of a lawyer friend for this. Neither he nor I charged the client.

◻ Saved client 10% excise tax, $1,300, on distribution from her mutual fund IRA by informing her of the permanent disability exception, and provided proper tax forms and IRS documents to back it.

◻ Advised client to dollar cost average into the market $1,100,000 10/3/07 when the Dow Jones Industrial Average (DJIA) was at 13,968. By March 27, 2008, the DJIA had dropped to 12,303 down 11.92% or 1,665 points but the portfolio was down just 1.68%, saving some $100,000 in potential losses.

◻ Helped a client find lower cost securities bond insurance than the standard 3%, which would save him thousands of dollars for his BP stock.

◻ Saved client $420,000 by stopping a fraudulent attempt to wire money out of account.

After reading all of these, please understand that I am not bragging. Most advisors have scores of stories like these. The media, which is mostly critical and dismissive of investment advisors, will rarely talk about the extras that advisors provide. They want their readers to believe that all advisors care about are fees and commissions. (This also manipulates readers into believing that the media is more valuable than it is.) This is far from the truth. Much of what advisors do for clients has nothing to do with selling them investments and earning a commission.

Instead, industry studies show that the average investment advisor spends most of his or her time on helping you rather than selling you. One such study by Prince and Associates, Inc. and New River found that of the five major advisor activities—1) relationship management, 2) prospecting and selling, 3) portfolio management, 4) professional development, and 5) administrative matters—advisors spend most time on administrative matters.[26] Prospecting and selling was number three.

Hire an advisor.

Don't Chase Returns, Chase Odds:
Diversify—But Diversify Wisely and Widely

> My ventures are not in one bottom trusted,
> Nor to one place; nor is my whole estate
> Upon the fortune of this present year.
> Therefore my merchandise makes me not sad.
> —William Shakespeare,
> *The Merchant of Venice*

After five days (chapters) you may now believe me when I say that stocks are less risky than bonds. But this is only because you know that I mean that balanced against long-term retirement income needs, you have a greater chance of reaching your objectives if you invest in stocks. But you also are a student of the market and know that, just as it did in 2008, the stock market can drop by 37% (the S&P 500, in this case) or more in one year.

So what do you do? What is an actionable way to successful investing? I believe the key is to get odds in your favor. The best way to do that, in my opinion, is to diversify your investments. As venerable money manager Dimensional Fund Advisors says:

"Diversification is the most essential tool available to investors. It enables them to capture broad market forces while reducing the excess, uncompensated risk arising in individual stocks."[1] And Nick Murray, prolific speaker and author, gives an interesting definition of diversification: "Diversification is the conscious decision never to be able to make a killing, in return for the priceless blessing of never getting killed."[2] This is the essence of "seeking lower returns" of which I spoke in Day 3.

A wealthy friend told me that diversification is just "five ways to lose money." He was joking and doesn't practice this in real life, as he owns property all over the world. He lives in a beautiful modern home in Zurich, owns a penthouse condo in the Four Seasons in Atlanta, and has another spacious home in Franklin, Tennessee. In addition he owns scores of commercial properties. When he crosses the Atlantic to return home, he does so in a first-class berth on the *Queen Mary*. How? Diversification is the reason he lives as well as he does.

Mark Cuban, the colorful billionaire and owner of the Dallas Mavericks said in a *Wall Street Journal* interview that "[d]iversification is for idiots."[3] Cuban owns stocks, options, bonds, MLPs, GNMAs, real estate, a popular television show, multiple businesses, IPOs, and of course an NBA basketball team. See the irony yet?

The Original Diversification Model

What is diversification? The basic model for diversification is two investments rather than just one investment. It is easy to visualize two investments in which one goes up while the other one goes down. Got it? You are now diversified. Diversification in the securities world was essentially invented by Walter L. Morgan (1898–1998), a CPA in Pennsylvania, in 1928. Morgan managed an active accounting practice and believed the idea of forming a mutual fund would help his clients to invest in a portfolio of stocks and not be burdened by clipping coupons from multiple bonds.

The fund was called Industrial and Power Securities Company and was later renamed the Wellington Fund in 1935, for the Duke of Wellington. The objectives of the fund were: 1) conservation of capital, 2) reasonable current income, and 3) profits without undue risk. The balanced fund of stocks, bonds, and cash helped investors navigate through the most turbulent period in market history. (See Figure 6-1.)

Figure 6-1

There could not have been a worse time to start a stock mutual fund, or perhaps a better time to start a balanced fund. The Dow Jones Industrial Average (DJIA) peaked at 381.17 on September 3, 1929, and lost 90% of its value over the next three years to reach a low of 41.22 on July 8, 1932. In contrast, the Wellington Fund lost 58.5%. The DJIA finally closed again above its previous high at 382.74 on November 23, 1954. The Wellington Fund earned a 5.9% annual return during this fateful 25-year period.

In 1974 the Vanguard Group was formed by John Bogle; the Wellington Fund became a charter member. In 1977 the Wellington Management Company board permanently adopted the approximate 65% U.S. stocks/35% U.S. bonds. There were only eight other mutual funds in existence in 1929; today the Vanguard Wellington Fund Investor Shares is by far the largest and most successful of those original funds. I believe that what Morgan created—this "balanced" fund with a fixed combination of stocks and bonds—is the most durable investment strategy ever built. He is my hero, and incidentally gave John Bogle, the founder of Vanguard, his start.

Does Diversification Work?

How has the original diversification model done more recently? Figure 6-2 may surprise you. The original diversification model outperformed the first S&P 500 Index fund. For the entirety of the life of the S&P 500 Index fund (inception date August 31, 1976), the balanced (two assets) fund outpaced the one-asset fund, and did so with less risk. And, for all of those whose answer to every investment question is "lower cost," note that the balanced fund expense ratio is more than 50% higher than the stock fund expense ratio. None of these returns are guaranteed into the future, but I want you to see a very real example of the potential benefits of diversification on the most basic level.

The Original Diversification Model[4]

	100% Stocks	Balanced
Annual Return	11.1%	11.2%
$10,000 =	$547,798	$570,933
10-year beta	1.00	0.64
12-month yield	−43.3%	−28.7%
Worst 1 year	−16.1%	−5.8%
Worst 3 years, annual	−3.5%	3.5%
Worst 10 years, annual	1.7%	2.3%
Gross Expense Ratio	0.17	0.26

Figure 6-2

A re Two Assets Enough?

In 1929 the securities markets recognized two asset classes: stocks and bonds. Since then, through securitization, we are able to invest in the worlds' oldest investable assets (real estate and commodities) using stocks, mutual funds, ETFs, and other means. When you add cash, or money market funds, you see that there are actually then five major investable asset classes: stocks, bonds, cash, real estate, and commodities. As Maurice Sendak said, "There must be more to life than having everything." With investing *everything* is stocks, bonds, cash, real estate, and commodities.

You need all of them in your portfolio: stocks for long-term capital appreciation, bonds for income, real estate for more income and growth, commodities as an inflation hedge, and cash to absorb the effects of market movements. I call this moving from black and white diversification (stocks and bonds) to color diversification. Since 2008 I have calculated the total value of all major investable assets.

You can see in Figure 6-3 that the first person to $240 trillion wins, as this is the total value of all investable assets.

Total Assets [5]		
Asset Class	Value	% of total
Stocks	$66.0	27%
Bonds	$104.7	43%
Cash	$2.7	1%
Real Estate	$50.4	21%
Commodities	$19.0	8%
Total	$242.8 Trillion	

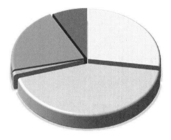

Figure 6-3

Note that commodities and real estate make up almost 30% of the value of total investable assets. As such they are not "alternative investments," as many investment professionals call them, but are essential portfolio components. In fact, in the 20 years ended 2014, commodities and real estate were likelier than U.S. stocks and bonds to be the top one or two asset classes. These returns, of course, are not guaranteed to continue, as each of these asset classes swap leadership over time, but you would have missed something valuable if you did not own them.

How Does Diversification Reduce Risk?

Remember in Day 3 when I talked about the relative advantage of *not* losing 4% rather than making 4%, and how that magically can give you a higher return? Can diversification help us reduce those negative returns without significantly reducing the positive returns? Yes. Figure 6-4 shows a comparison of the five assets (stocks, bonds, cash, real estate, and commodities), only now expanded to seven assets by dividing stocks and bonds into U.S. and non–U.S. Now we have U.S. and non–U.S. stocks, U.S. and non U.S.–bonds, cash, real estate, and commodities. How have they compared against 100% U.S. stocks, and 60% U.S. stocks/40% U.S. bonds (the traditional balanced model) since 1970?[6]

Major 7 Assets Equally Weighted vs. Stocks and Balanced

Category	Average Return %	Standard Deviation
S&P 500	10.5	17.2
60/40	9.7	11.2
7 Assets Equally Weighted	9.7	8.1

Figure 6-4

Notice that the returns were roughly similar but the standard deviation (a measure of variation of returns, or volatility) dropped dramatically as you moved from one asset (S&P 500), to two assets (60/40), to seven assets. Why does this matter? It matters because, even though you would have made more money in stocks at the very end of this 45-year period, 70% of the time the seven-asset portfolio was worth *more* than the 100% stock portfolio. This is a potential key benefit of diversification.

Diversification as Risk Management

As you know, I do not believe that risk equals reward. There are many ways to manage risk: tactically move assets around based on a technical or fundamental preference (such as we will buy stocks when the P/E multiple is below the historic average), move to 100% cash when certain momentum indicators are triggered, hedge using options or futures, and so forth. My way (which thousands of advisors, investors, and I learned from my business partner Craig Israelsen) is to equally weigh multiple low-correlated assets. The seven assets represent this basic strategy. There may be no best way to manage investment risk, but I believe that this is one of the best ways to *automatically* manage investment risks.

Here's a way to understand how this works. Figure 6-5 shown on page 193 shows a vexing chart that I have shown my clients for years. Most of them look at me quizzically and wonder quite how this is possible.

Note that both portfolios have an average return of 7%. (This illustration is not dependent on earning 7%, nor is the 7% guaranteed in either portfolio.) The point is that even if you earn the same average return with the diversified portfolio that you earn with the single-asset portfolio, you have the greater chance of making more money in the diversified portfolio with five different investments than the single-asset portfolio. You could end up with investments that underperformed the 7%, too—which is why there is no guarantee that this will work in every market condition.

Would You Rather Get 7% or a 7% Return?

Value	Return	Asset	15 Years
Fixed Account			
$50,000	7%	Fund A	$137,951
Diversified Portfolio			
$10,000	0%	Fund B	$10,000
$10,000	5%	Fund C	$20,789
$10,000	8%	Fund D	$31,721
$10,000	10%	Fund E	$41,772
$10,000	12%	Fund F	$54,735
$50,000	Average 7%		$159,017

Returns are not guaranteed and do not represent any particular investment. Diversification does not guarantee a higher return and/or lower risk.

Figure 6-5

To be clear, does diversification guarantee greater returns or lower losses? No. There are periods in the market where single assets like U.S. stocks, gold, high-tech stocks, emerging markets, and so forth, go on a run, and the diversified investor looks like a stamp collector quietly admiring his portfolio under a magnifying glass and losing out on all the action.

Alternatively, the market can drop and a diversified portfolio seems to just sink with it. The fourth quarter of 2008 is a good example. However, don't lose heart; diversification may be a key to preserving and growing capital for the long-term investor. Don't be too worried about getting it exactly right. As Don Phillips of Morningstar, Inc. said about market activity, "Change is constant, but change is not random."[7] This means that there are certain patterns, strategies, and methods to market activity. Diversification is one of those strategies that is likely to work—and remember: This is all about getting odds in your favor.

Diversifying Means Control

When the odds are in your favor, you, not the investment, are in control. You can't control the market but you can control the downside, or at least reduce it. Control what you can control, and forget about the rest. You cannot control the pluses, but you can control the minuses. This is one of the automatic benefits that diversifying can make: You are there when the markets go up, but more protected when they drop because you own many low-correlated investments.

The Costs of Not Diversifying

Before I continue with the virtues of diversifying let me give you three harsh reminders of what happens to you when you *don't* diversify: Enron, Madoff, and Japan. If you had 100% of your 401(k) in Enron stock, or 100% of your net worth with Bernie Madoff, or 100% of your money in Japan (for the last 25 years), you are in bad shape. But, you need to recognize these as diversification problems, not as inherent weaknesses with investing.

Enron was not a corporate malfeasance problem for investors. Lack of diversification was the problem. Bernie Madoff's dishonesty was not why investors are now penniless. Lack of diversification was. Japan's lost decade (actually two decades plus) was not the problem. Lack of diversification was the problem. Japan is only one country. Why would you have all your savings with one country? Are you seeing a pattern?

Most stories about investors ruined in the market are stories about lack of diversification. The Enron story is a classic where the stock went from $90 to $0 in 331 trading days and finally died in 2001. But that's not the story. According to *Dun & Bradstreet,* nearly 100,000 businesses fail yearly in the United States.[8] Two hundred fifty-seven public companies with $258 billion in assets declared bankruptcy in 2001, the same year that Enron collapsed.[9] There are approximately 15,000 publicly traded companies, 9,000 of which are the major public companies listed in *The Corporate Directory* from Walker's Research. Therefore approximately 2% of public companies fail every year. This is why you diversify.

For those who had 5% of their portfolios with Enron, Madoff, or Japan, the losses are simply reminders to diversify. For those who wagered 100% on these, let their misfortune serve as a warning to you. (I guess you could have put 33% in Madoff, Enron, and Japan so diversification does not always work!)

Diversify everything. Diversify asset classes (stocks, bonds, commodities, real estate, money markets, etc.), product types (securities, mutual funds, variable annuities, hard assets, etc.), and custodians (banks, brokerage firms, insurance companies, etc.).

When I say to diversify, I mean it. Every sad story in my business starts with "I gave him everything, and then..." or "I put all I had into X and then...." I know this sounds defeatist, but I agree with Dr. Quincy Krosby, chief market strategist for Prudential Annuities, who said, "I want my portfolio to be covered for whatever may happen. We are not in control of our destiny anymore, so I want to be diversified no matter what kind of market we are in."[10] Next, record all of your holdings on one spreadsheet. On that spreadsheet you should see a variety of 800 numbers, financial institutions, account numbers, advisors, asset types, and so forth. Your advisor should help you with this. Successful country-western singer Willie Nelson went bankrupt in 1990. To pay off the IRS (which he did in three years) he devoted all of his earnings from an album called *The IRS Tapes: Who'll Buy My Memories?*[11] Nelson said in an article that the key to his comeback was to compile all of his holdings on one page. This better managed the complications and confusion from his vast estate. Since reading that, I have reduced my clients' holdings to one page for the same reason.

How Much Should I Put in Each Asset?

Figure 6-6 (with a nod of thanks to Callan Associates, Inc. for creating this pictorial teaching style, which they call the *periodic table of investments*) compares the seven assets described previously for 10-year returns through 2014. Each of the seven assets is ranked in order from top to bottom the highest to lowest annual returns.

Annual Returns Ranked in Order of 7 Assets (2005–2014)[12]

2005	2006	2007	2008	2009	2010	2011	2012	2013	2014
Commod 31.97%	Real Estate 35.97%	Commod 32.59%	US Bonds 10.43%	Non US Stocks 31.78%	Real Estate 28.07%	Real Estate 9.37%	Non US Stocks 17.32%	US Stocks 32.39%	Real Estate 32.00%
Real Estate 13.82%	Non US Stocks 26.34%	Non US Stocks 11.17%	Non US Bonds 9.48%	Real Estate 28.46%	Commod 11.93%	US Bonds 7.90%	Real Estate 17.12%	Non US Stocks 23.29%	US Stocks 13.69%
Non US Stocks 13.54%	Commod 16.98%	Non US Bonds 10.93%	Cash 1.51%	US Stocks 26.50%	US Stocks 11.71%	Non US Bonds 5.24%	US Stocks 16.00%	Real Estate 1.22%	US Bonds 5.97%
US Stocks 4.91%	US Stocks 15.79%	US Bonds 8.47%	Commod -30.94%	Commod 16.35%	Non US Bonds 6.12%	US Stocks 1.19%	US Bonds 4.22%	Cash 0.05%	Cash 0.02%
Cash 3.34%	Non US Bonds 7.29%	US Stocks 5.49%	US Stocks -37.00%	US Bonds 5.93%	Non US Stocks 2.57%	Cash 0.06%	Commod 4.16%	US Bonds -2.02%	Non US Bonds -2.77%
US Bonds 1.68%	Cash 5.07%	Cash 4.77%	Real Estate -39.20%	Non US Bonds 4.36%	US Bonds 1.54%	Commod -2.39%	Non US Bonds 1.76%	Non US Bonds -4.88%	Non US Stocks -4.48%
Non US Bonds -8.81%	US Bonds 3.84%	Real Estate -17.56%	Non US Stocks -43.38%	Cash 0.15%	Cash 0.13%	Non US Stocks -12.26%	Cash 0.08%	Commod -6.92%	Commod -33.06%

- U.S. Stocks (Standard & Poor's 500 Index)
- Non-U.S. Stocks (MSCI EAFE Index)
- U.S. Bonds (Barclays Cap Aggregate Bond Index)
- Non-U.S. Bonds (Barclays Cap Global Treasury ex-US Index)
- Cash (3-Month Treasury Bills)
- Real Estate (Dow Jones US Select REIT TR Index)
- Commodities (Commod.) (DB LIQ Comm TR Index)*   *2014 only - Standard & Poor's GSCI TR Index

Figure 6-6

The first lesson is that the top-performing asset class is usually not the same every year. The second lesson is that the chart stops with the last full year of returns (in this case 2014). What does that tell you? It tells me that those who compiled the chart did not know what the numbers would be for the following year and beyond. Therefore, what is obvious is that the best-performing assets classes are variable and you cannot predict the future. As an investor, how should you use this information?

First, invest in multiple asset classes for the opportunity to hold the best performers, and so you will not hold *only* the worst-performing asset. Think of it this way: If you hold 20% each of these five major asset classes (stocks, bonds, cash, real estate, and commodities) you are guaranteed to *not* have 80% of your assets in the worst category.

The second is that if you do not know the future, what better way to invest than to equally weight?

Here is an example. Let's assume that you were so excited about U.S. stocks after a return of 33% in 1997 (not shown in Figure 6-6) that you invested 100% of your money into U.S. stocks. In 1998 stocks were up 29%. So far, so good. In 1999 stocks again were up 21%. You are still looking pretty smart, and have decided market timing works when you are as talented as you. Then, to your shock, for the next three years U.S. stocks returned –9%, –12%, and –22% respectively. Your $10,000 investment is now worth $9,710 after five years with 100% in U.S. stocks.

What if, instead of investing 100% in U.S. stocks, you decided to diversify at the end of 1997? You divide your $10,000 into the seven assets in Figure 6-6. Your returns from 1998 through 2002 would have been roughly 4%, 12%, 11%, –6%, and 4%. Your $10,000 would have grown to $12,640 after five years.[13] (See Figure 6-7.)

Diversity After a Strong Market Performance

Year	Diversified Portfolio		U.S Stocks	
1997	7.99%		33.36%	
1998	3.56%	$10,356	28.57%	$12,857
1999	12.32%	$11,632	21.05%	$15,563
2000	10.96%	$12,907	–9.11%	$14,146
2001	–5.98%	$12,136	–11.88%	$12,465
2002	**4.18%**	**$12,643**	**–22.10%**	**$9,710**

Assumption: Invest $10,000 after 1997 in U.S. Stocks (S&P 500) versus seven equally weighted assets (Diversified Portfolio). Past performance is no guarantee of future returns. Indexes are not investable.

Figure 6-7

Or, what if you chose "Non–U.S. Stocks" as your sole investment after the 31.8% return in 2009 (shown in Figure 6-6)? If you invested 100% at the end of 2009 into "Non–U.S. Stocks," five years later you would have been up 32.6% overall, and lost money in 2011 and 2014. Had you instead equally weighted the seven assets you would have been up 36.9% and never lost money in the five year period.[14]

There are many scenarios in which the numbers would not work out like this, but I believe that you have a better chance of improving your risk-adjusted returns by diversifying than by attempting to pick next year's winners from last year's list. But, even if you do not improve your current returns, you may reduce your risk, and I think by now you realize how important it is to reduce risk.

Equally weighting your investments is a suggested model. But be advised, as Thomas Wilson, chief insurance risk officer of ING Group remarked, "A model is always wrong, but not useless."[15] In other words, there are always better ways to choose how to invest *after* the fact. However, I have found that when you use a model and are broadly diversified, you don't have to think much about the market, may experience less volatility, and therefore will not be as emotionally or financially at risk.

The Chart That Changed My Life

Figure 6-8 shows the best one-picture illustration of the benefits of diversification that I have seen in more than 30 years in the investment industry. It is from an article written by Eleanor Laise in the *Wall Street Journal* on January 16, 2008 that illustrates the research of Craig Israelsen, PhD, who was then a professor at Brigham Young University.[16] As you can see, the investor starts with large and small U.S. stocks, then adds in equal weights foreign stocks, U.S. bonds, cash, REITs (real estate investment trusts), and commodities. Also assumed are 5% withdrawals, which increase by 3% per year.

Over the 37-year time period you can see that the returns were stable, but the real story is the dramatic drop in the standard deviation and the worst year's decline in value as you added assets. Standard deviation (volatility) fell by half, and the worst year's decline in value dropped by almost 70%. This is significant risk reduction. An investment advisor's job is either to increase returns or reduce risk. This seemed to be a way to do it. I e-mailed Craig Israelsen that day to introduce myself, and we later built a company off of his 7Twelve™ strategy. The 7Twelve strategy has become one of the most popular investment strategies in the country, with thousands of advisors and investors eagerly using it. This is why it changed my life.

The Importance of Diversification[17]

Asset	Aggregate Annual Rate of Return	Standard Deviation	Worst Year Decline*
Large cap and small cap U.S. stocks	10.7%	18.0%	–30.8%
Add foreign stocks to above portfolio	10.9%	17.2%	–29.8%
Add U.S. intermediate term bonds to above	10.6%	13.0%	–22.0%
Add cash to above	10.0%	10.5%	–16.9%
Add REITs to above	10.4%	10.6%	–18.8%
Add commodies to above	11.3%	8.7%	–10.2%

*Includes annual withdrawal.

Figure 6-8

To fully implement this strategy you can see in Figure 6-9 the 7 assets and how they are sub-divided into *twelve* assets or funds underneath—7Twelve.

The 7Twelve™ Strategy
Approximately 65% in Equities and Diversifying Assets

U.S. Stocks	Non-U.S. Stocks	Real Estate	Commodities
Large Companies	Developed Markets	REITs	Natural Resources
Medium Companies	Emerging Markets		Commodities
Small Companies			

Approximately 35% in Fixed Income and Cash

U.S. Bonds	Non-U.S. Bonds	Cash
Aggregate Bonds	International Bonds	U.S. Money Markets
TIPS		

Figure 6-9

I recommend that when you think in terms of an investment model that you consider this as a start. This model is *b*alanced for durability, *i*ndexed for cost effectiveness and accountability, *p*assively (or strategically) managed so you do not have to tinker with it, *e*qually weighted, so you do not have to try to predict the market, and *d*iversified into all major asset classes. Think b-i-p-e-d—two feet. This is one way to put two solid and steady feet under your portfolio.

Back-testing, index to index, this 12-asset balanced model has generally shown outperformance of the two-asset model (60% U.S. stocks/40% U.S. bonds) for long periods, though there is no guarantee that this will continue. To be clear: This is not investment advice—only a template. The key is for you and your advisor to find the right mix of investments for your risk tolerances and investment objectives.

Stocks vs. Mutual Funds

What about diversification inside the asset classes? I am surprised to see how much some people invest in single stocks when diversification is so easy. You see this often in retirement plans in which the company match is paid in stock or in stock option plans. It's not so bad to receive stock as a match if you monitor and sell it occasionally to make sure that you are not over-weighted in the stock. As a rule of thumb, you are over-weighted in any stock that the loss of which would make a significant difference in your life.

Another way to diversify is within mutual funds and variable annuities. Both cost more than owning individual stocks (unless you are holding your stocks in a fee-based account); however, the higher cost can give you:

1. Exposure to more than just a few stocks.

2. Professional management.

3. Automatic tax lot accounting.

4. Customer service.

5. Automatic investing and distribution options.

6. The ability to make lower cost switches
   between investments and investment strategies.

David L. Martin, an expert in bank mergers and acquisitions, and former managing director of Sandler O'Neill, told me, "I'll tell you the one thing you need to know about investing, it will fit on one page, never buy individual stocks."[18] I do not think I could build a better case than that for mutual funds.

If you are opposed to mutual funds for some reason or enjoy making your own stock selections you can create a diversified portfolio with individual stock selections as long as you select enough and over a broad range of industries. According to Daniel J. Burnside, PhD, CFA, "As a rule of thumb, diversifiable risk will be reduced by the following amounts."[19]

- Holding 25 stocks reduces diversifiable risk by about 80%.

- Holding 100 stocks reduces diversifiable risk by about 90%.

- Holding 400 stocks reduces diversifiable risk by about 95%.

You can control capital gains with stocks easier than you can with mutual funds. Mutual funds have to declare capital gains and pay them out; stocks do not. As you can see there are advantages to both. The choice depends on your personal situation. This is another reason why you need an advisor to help make the right decision for you.

The Bonds That Tie

I have spent a lot of time illustrating the difference in returns between stocks and bonds. Because of this you may believe that I am against bonds. In truth, bonds are vital to your well-being and are an excellent diversifier in a portfolio. Remember that they were 40% of the two-asset portfolio that beat the S&P 500 since 1976 that I recently mentioned.

Part of the reason why I have spent so much time on stocks is because you already buy bonds (or certificate of deposit, money markets, etc.) and don't need me to sell you on them: "The U.S. bond markets total about $40 trillion, twice the size of the approximately $19 trillion U.S. stock market."[20]

To attempt to cleverly describe the difference between stocks and bonds, I would like to introduce you to Richard P. Woltman. Woltman is a founder of the independent broker-dealer industry. His broker-dealers were acquired by SunAmerica (later AIG Financial Advisors) and RCS Capital. There is probably no individual in the independent broker-dealer industry that has had a bigger influence than Richard Woltman. Mr. Woltman said, "The investment business is a lot like art. There are many ways to express yourself."[21] I appreciate his sentiment, as it adds verve to an otherwise mechanical industry.

Similarly, some say that *stocks are an art, and bonds are a science.* Bonds have par values, maturity dates, fixed coupon (interest) rates, senior claims on assets, and inherent guarantees. Some are even insured. Bonds are a science because their price movements can be predicted more accurately than stocks. And frankly, you need some science in your portfolio. Therefore, I created what I believe is the first fully diversified equally weighted bond portfolio called the *3Twelve*™ *Total Bond*. The *3* is for the types of bonds (represented by the medium gray shades in Figure 6-10): government, corporate, and mortgage). The *Twelve* sub-divides these into equally weighted categories. It is a happy coincidence, but only a coincidence that like 7Twelve (created by Craig Israelsen) there are 12 major categories.

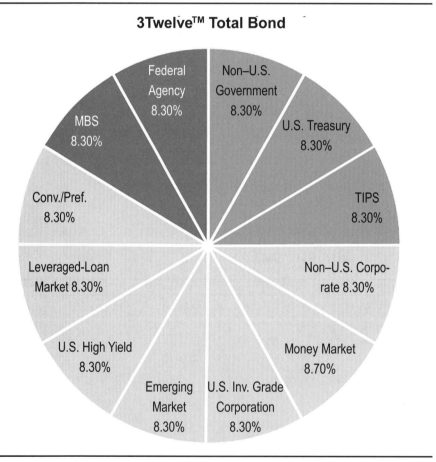

3Twelve™ Total Bond

Figure 6-10

Figure 6-10 shows what the 3Twelve™ Total Bond looks like in one picture.

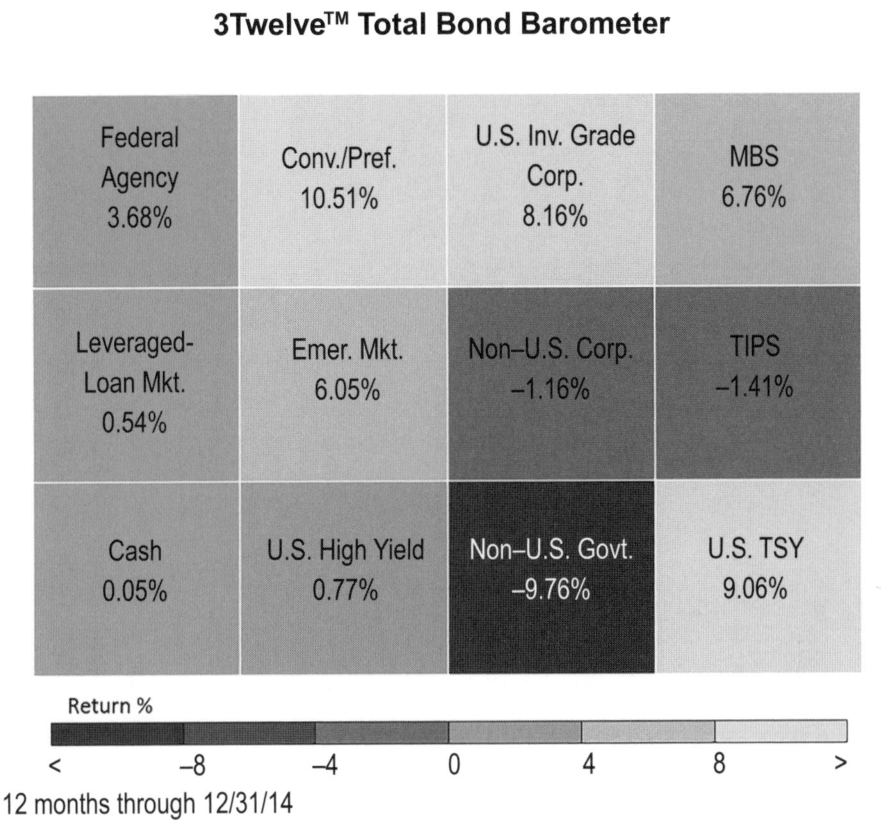

3Twelve™ Total Bond Barometer

Federal Agency 3.68%	Conv./Pref. 10.51%	U.S. Inv. Grade Corp. 8.16%	MBS 6.76%
Leveraged-Loan Mkt. 0.54%	Emer. Mkt. 6.05%	Non–U.S. Corp. –1.16%	TIPS –1.41%
Cash 0.05%	U.S. High Yield 0.77%	Non–U.S. Govt. –9.76%	U.S. TSY 9.06%

Return %

<   –8   –4   0   4   8   >

12 months through 12/31/14

Figure 6-11

Figure 6-11 illustrates why 3Twelve tends to work. Note the significant dispersion of returns among the 12 bond types[22] from a low of –9.76% to a high of 10.51% in the chart. This gives the portfolio a low correlation, which means that you have a well-diversified portfolio instead of 12 bond classes that act similarly. The correlation was less than .40 for the

10-year period ending 2014. Correlation of 1.00 is perfect posi-tive correlation and a correlation of –1.00 is perfect negative correlation. Therefore, .40 suggests low correlation, which is the key to diversification.[23]

What problem does 3Twelve attempt to solve? A big fear for bond investors is buying a 20-year long-term bond, say, with a fixed interest rate (called a coupon) and then, sud-denly, experiencing an interest rate rise. When this happens the same bond that this investor bought is now available with a higher coupon, so his or her bond is instantly worth less money in the secondary market.

However, if instead, the investor put his or her money into the three-asset core (equally weighted), it would have outper-formed U.S. Treasury bonds in each of the five periods from 1980 to 1999 that interest rates increased by more than 2%. For the rising rate periods from 1998 to 1999, and from 2003 to 2006, the 3Twelve[TM] Total Bond outperformed Treasury bonds and other standard bond benchmarks.[24]

Even investment professionals are surprised to learn that diversification works just as well for bonds as it does for stocks. A full discussion of either the 7Twelve or 3Twelve investment strategies are beyond the scope of this book, but I wanted to give you an introduction to a broader and deeper concept of diversification than you have likely seen. And again, I must remind you that both of these are only models. My message is not *Use these models*; my message is *Find the right model with your advisor*—but do find a model.

Heads You Win, Tails You Win

Here is another way to get the odds in your favor. Princeton University Professor Burton Malkiel found that the S&P 500 beat 70% of all equity managers retained by pension plans over the 1975–1994 20-year periods. Another study by Robert Kirby, former chairman of Capital Guardian, indicated that out of 115 U.S. equity mutual funds that were in business for 30 years or more, only 41 (36%) beat the S&P 500 index, and only 23 of the funds (20%) beat the index by 1% per year or more. Seventy-four of the funds (64%) failed to produce a record equal to the S&P 500's 10.25% return since 1961. And, using information from CDA/Cadence, Tweedy, Browne Company, LLC found that over the December 31, 1981–December 31, 1994, 13-year period, the S&P 500 beat 81% of the surviving equity mutual funds.[25]

Finally, Standard & Poor's was even more definitive when they reported, "The only consistent data point we have observed over a five-year horizon is that a majority of active equity and bond managers in most categories lag comparable benchmark indices."[26] However, during the five-year period ended 2008, the average large value and large blend stock fund beat the passive S&P 500 index.[27] That is, in a bad market active management outperformed passive management, so I would caution you against being so doctrinaire that you only invest in indexes.

Indexing is a way to get the odds in your favor—that is, unless it's not. Aren't these contradictory opinions? No—not if you diversify. You never know when active management is going to outperform passive management or vice versa, therefore just as you need stocks, bonds, cash, real estate, and commodities, you also need active and passive management in your portfolio. Once again, if in doubt always use the more diversified approach.

Seatbacks to Upright Position, Tray Tables Locked: Prepare to Land

As we approach the end, I'd like to share a few more important notes. First, *past performance is no guarantee of future return.* You see this expression a lot in the investment business. Most of the investment returns figures in this book came from the U.S. markets in the 20th century. The 20th century was a great century for the American stock market. The Dow began at 66.61 in 1900 (January 3, 1900) and ended the century (December 29, 2000) at 10,787.99. The appreciation alone was 6.8% average annual return. The average dividend rate compounded at about 4%, which would yield a total return of more than 10% yearly. This is significantly higher than bonds and inflation. I would challenge anyone to find a higher returning "passive" investment.

What about non–U.S. markets? "Take Japan, please," to paraphrase Henny Youngman. What a disaster Japan is. None of what I have said in this book is true for Japan. Japan is a socialist, centrally planned, command economy. What's unsettling about this is that Japan is the world's third-largest economy by GDP according to the International Monetary Fund.[28] It was second largest in 2008. Growth and socialism are bitter opponents. The Nikkei's (Japan's benchmark index) all time high was 38,915.87, where it closed on December 29, 1989. It is now, 20-plus years later, trading at less than half of that level. It may be the world's only equity market that needs a reverse split. It is a 25-year-old story and startles me every time I think about it. Japan is a resounding unmistakable demand to diversify. In November 2008, I asked Bill Spitz, former manager of the endowment for Vanderbilt University, whom I introduced earlier, when will Japan's equity markets recover? His answer was the most definitive of any answer that any money manager has ever given. He replied, "Never. Japan is incapable of reform."[29]

The Future of Money

It's a shame. We were so obsessed with the end of the millennia, which was really nothing more than a numerological oddity, and the hokum of Y2K, that we missed the bigger story, which was the end of the century. The end of the millennia was a geological event, but the end of the century was a generational event: The setting moon eclipsed the setting sun. Author Harold Evans called the 20th century—more specifically the period between 1889 (the settling of the frontier) and 1989 (the inauguration of George Bush)—"The American Century."

I mention these facts about the power of the U.S. market in the 20th century and Japan's weakness to suggest that you not make assumptions about the future that do not include that you could be entirely wrong. I want you to be successful even when you are wrong, so diversify.

Also, don't forget about politicians. They can ruin this. Many in this country are whether they know it or not. Risk-averse former Senator Barney Frank intoned against investing any of Social Security assets in stocks, but became recklessly fearless with Fannie Mae and Freddie Mac when he recommend that we "roll the dice" and double down on government's commitment to these institutions that became the lenders of last resort to millions of insolvent American homeowners. What followed was the worst recession in modern history. So, it's not that senators are reluctant to gamble, it is that they gamble on the wrong things. After all, these are the people that brought us state lotteries and casinos, both terrible investments, and are much to blame for the permanent poverty class that befalls generations of lower-middle-class Americans.

Or look at the difference between how one president versus another president handled risk. When the space shuttle *Challenger* exploded in mid-air, President Ronald Reagan described it thus:

> I know it's hard to understand, but sometimes painful things like this happen. It's all part of the process of exploration and discovery. It's all part of taking a chance and expanding man's horizons. The future doesn't belong to the fainthearted; it belongs to the brave. The *Challenger* crew was pulling us into the future, and we'll continue to follow them. I've always had great faith in and respect for our space program. And what happened today does nothing to diminish it.

We don't hide our space program. We don't keep secrets and cover things up. We do it all up front and in public. That's the way freedom is, and we wouldn't change it for a minute. We'll continue our quest in space. There will be more shuttle flights and more shuttle crews and, yes, more volunteers, more civilians, more teachers in space. Nothing ends here; our hopes and our journeys continue.[30]

Contrast that with President Barack Obama's handling of the BP Gulf of Mexico oil spill in 2010, starting with his interior secretary Ken Salazar's threatening, "We will keep our boot on their neck until the job gets done."[31] Obama's remarks included:

Already, this oil spill is the worst environmental disaster America has ever faced.... Tomorrow, I will meet with the chairman of BP and inform him that he is to set aside whatever resources are required to compensate the workers and business owners who have been harmed as a result of his company's recklessness.... Already, I've issued a six-month moratorium on deep water drilling.[32]

This incident was just the beginning of a political retreat from oil exploration, and it was perilous for jobs and the economy. One president assured the country that risk is a part of life and we need to press on. Another warned us that some risks are too great and that we should cower from them. When investors cower by moving everything into money market funds and CDs after the stock market drops 20%, they do the same thing. Their unwillingness to accept and to manage risk is actually a greater risk than pressing on. Though it is true that risk does not equal reward, understanding and managing risks, instead of running from them, can bring great rewards. And, as we have seen, risks are functions of opportunities, not just the worst that can happen.

However, let's not overestimate the rewards, either. I am not trying to sell you 20th-century returns in the 21st century. My theory is that the stock market will only outperform bonds, not that it will produce a 10% long-term annual rate of return. If bond rates stay at 2%, then stocks can double bonds' returns with a mere 4% return. Even if stocks return their historical premium over stocks, which is about 3–4%, we are still just talking about 5–6% returns in stocks. Is their precedent for such a dreary outlook? Yes. Back to Japan. In Japan, interest rates have dropped and stayed low, the population is aging with no sign of a turnaround, savings rates have dropped accordingly, and the stock market has responded as expected.

These myriad problems are best handled not by making bold predictions but by diversifying. Diversification is the shield against nearly everything that is attacking your future.

Now What?

I hope that I have built the case that:

1. Risk ≠ reward.
2. Stocks are less risky than bonds long term.

3. Reduce negative returns.

4. Predict yourself, not the stock market.

5. Hire an advisor.

6. Diversify.

If you agree with what you have read here then take this book to your existing advisor and ask him or her to apply it to your portfolio. If you do not have an advisor now, you have enough of a personal investment philosophy and sufficient motivation to ask the right questions to hire the right advisor. Whichever is the case, please start now. "Touch has a memory," wrote John Keats. The longer you wait, the greater your chance of forgetting some of these themes and back you will be to where you were. Intentional investors win; the rest depend on luck. And remember: Bad luck (not good luck) is embedded into the market because the math is against you. To win you need to act differently.

Caution: This book, alone, is not investment advice. I am not saying that I am not an investment advisor. I am saying that I cannot give you proper investment advice anonymously through a book such as this. Nor is this book legal or tax advice. I have many friends who are lawyers and accountants, but that doesn't make me one. Before implementing any of these strategies, please consult with a professional credentialed investment advisor.

All returns herein are estimates and not guaranteed. Additionally, past performance does not guarantee future returns. I don't say this to protect myself or to hedge; I say this because it is true. Finally, there is no guarantee that using the investments and techniques described herein will yield a positive result for you. The investment markets are now and will always be an open system with no boundaries. Because there are infinite factors that determine securities prices, predictions about returns and outcomes are impossible.

I am confident that if you have thought carefully about these concepts and work to apply them in your investing life that your outcomes will improve. I wish for you nothing but good fortune.

On Money and Happiness

"It is better to have a permanent income than to be fascinating," said Oscar Wilde, but, can money buy happiness? A recent study cited by *The Economist* called "Subjective Well-Being and Income: Is There Any Evidence of Satiation?" by Betsey Stevenson and Justin Wolfers, says yes.[1] Gallup pollsters created a "satisfaction ladder" in which the top rung represented highest satisfaction. Those polled were asked how high they are on the ladder from zero to 10, and how much they earn. Most people around the world reported more satisfaction the richer they were. And there seems to be no point where the respondent plateaued. In other words, satisfaction and income seem to be related linearly—which may be why the wealthy people you know never seem to have enough.

They are satiated but are they happy? The meaning of the word *happiness* is mutable. The author of the shopworn expression *Money can't buy happiness* may have set us up and purposely picked a word with such liquid meaning that it could never be proven wrong.

However, substitute almost any other word (*comfort, health, security,* etc.) for *happiness* and the negative expression *Money can't buy happiness* is simply incorrect: Money can't buy *comfort.* Yes it can. Money can't buy *health.* Yes it can. Money can't buy *security.* Yes it can. If money cannot buy happiness, it certainly can buy a lot of other things. The reason I believe this is because I have seen it. I have seen it in the contrasting lives of my clients; my wealthier clients have options that less-wealthy ones do not. And, I have seen it in me.

Maybe we need a new expression, such as *Happiness is the only thing money* can't *buy* or *Money can't buy happiness—just everything else.*

Then, there is Oscar Wilde, again, who wrote in his play *A Woman of No Importance,* "Who, being loved, is poor?" Maybe this is the all-purpose retort to *Money cannot buy happiness.* Or, maybe it's Lee Iacocca, who lamented our sometimes-pathological fixation on money when he said, "I never in my lifetime saw so many people who are so affluent, yet so anxious. Is anybody happy anymore?"[2]

I think Craig Israelsen got closest to the essence of it when he said:

Consider this: money and wealth do not move with us through the veil of death, yet the skills attained through the righteous use of such resources are a permanent part of us. Temporal tasks that facilitate the development of spiritual characteristics such as patience, prioritizing, gratitude, self-mastery, self-reliance, and endurance are portable—and needed—beyond the grave.[3]

Yes. He said *beyond the grave.*

Accordingly, philosopher William James said, "The greatest use of life is to spend it for something that will outlast it."

Could there be a worthier use of our time and money?

Preface

1. Washington Mutual Investors Fund, form N-30D, April 30, 2001, *www.secinfo.com/d36De.4f89u.htm#1stPage.*

2. Investment Company Institute.

3. Thayer, PhD, Colette. "Preparation for Retirement: The Haves and Have-Nots." *AARP Knowledge Management,* 2007.

4. Wolff, PhD, Edward N. "The Asset Price Meltdown and the Wealth of the Middle Class." New York University, August 26, 2012.

5. Kendall, Stephanie, and Scott Stapf. "New Study: Typical American Household Has Net Financial Assets of $1,000," *www.consumerfed.org/pdfs/primerica.pdf.*

6. Engel, Rep. Eliot L., 17th District Bronx Office, New York, April 2005, *http://engel.house.gov/uploads/Social%20Security%20Mailing%20March%202005.pdf.*

7. Pethokoukis, James. "America's Bull Run," *U.S. News & World Reports,* January 4, 2008, *http://money.usnews.com/money/personal-finance/investing/articles/2008/01/04/americas-bull-run.*

Introduction

1. The DJIA's 8.36% rise for the week was the best since an 8.72% gain for the week ending October 8, 1982. March 21, 2003, *www.globalaffairs.org/forum/showthread.php?t=10342, http://query.nytimes.com/gst/fullpage.html?res=9C00E6DF1630F930A15750C0A9659C8B63.*

2. American Funds, Hypothetical Rolling Years Report, S&P 500 with Monthly Dividends, December 31, 1974–December 31, 1999, 25 years Rolling Periods, for period covering December 31,1927–December 31,2014. Copyright 2014 Thomson Reuters.

3. NASD (now FINRA) Investor Education Foundation, December 2004.

Day 1

1. Fleck, Carole. "Running Out of Money Worse Than Death," *AARP Bulletin,* July 1, 2010, *www.aarp.org/work/ retirement-planning/info-06-2010/running _ out _ of _ money _ worse _ than _ death.html.*

2. Blastland, Michael, and David Spiegelhalter. "Risk Is Never a Strict Numbers Game," *The Wall Street Journal,* July 18, 2014, *http://online.wsj.com/articles/ risk-is-never-a-strict-numbers-game-1405728892.*

3. University of Rochester Medical Center, *http://bit.ly/1jUx4j6.*

4. Breastcancer.org, February 23, 2013, *www.breastcancer.org/ treatment/surgery/risks/.*

5. Klevens, DDS, MPH, R. Monina, et al. "Estimating Health Care-Associated Infections and Deaths in U.S. Hospitals," 2002, *Public Health Reports* March–April 2007: Volume 122, *www.cdc.gov/hai/ pdfs/hai/infections_deaths.pdf.*

6. Society of Actuaries Annuity 2000 Mortality Table.

7. Damodaran, PhD, Aswath. "Historical Returns on Stocks, Bonds and Bills—United States," compiled by Andy Martin, December 31, 1927–December 31, 2013, *http://people.stern. nyu.edu/adamodar/New _ Home _ Page/home.htm.*

8. Gladwell, Malcolm. "The Sure Thing, How Entrepreneurs Really Succeed," *Annals of Business, New Yorker,* January 18, 2010.

9. Ibid.

10. Loomis, Carol. "Buffett Seeks a New Buffett," *Fortune Magazine,* March 21, 2007, *http://archive.fortune. com/2007/03/01/magazines/fortune/b _ newbuffett.fortune/ index.htm.*

11. "Undiscovered Managers," *Morningstar Advisor,* Spring 2008, page 62, *www.nxtbook.com/nxtbooks/morningstar/ advisor _ 2008spring/.*

12. Ibid.

13. Ibbotson Associates, Inc., March 1, 2002.

14. Morningstar, Inc. 10 years ending December 31, 2007.

15. Ibid.

16. Russel Kinnel, Morningstar, Inc. Average annual returns for 10 years ended December 31, 2009.

Day 2

1. American Funds Distributors, Inc., 1952 to April 2001 Stocks: S&P 500 With Dividends Reinvested, Savings Vehicles Composite, U.S. League of Savings Institutions, Federal Reserve Board, *www.secinfo.com/d36De.4f89u.htm.*

2. Damodaran, PhD, Aswath. December 31, 1927–December 31, 2014, S&P 500, 3-Month T-Bills.

3. American Funds Distributors, Inc., Hypothetical Illustration, S&P 500 With Monthly Dividends, December 31, 1927– December 31, 2014.

4. Damodaran, PhD, Aswath. S&P Composite vs. 10-Year Treasury Bonds, December 31, 1927–December 31, 2014, S&P 500 Dividends Not Reinvested, Rolling Averages (Geometric Mean Returns) calculated by author.

5. American Funds Distributors, Inc., Hypothetical Illustration, December 31, 1933–December 31, 2014, Dow Jones Industrial Average, T-Bill—3-Month Yield, Rolling 10-Year Periods. Best, Median, Worst: Stocks, 19.07%, 12.04%, .28%, T-Bills, 9.44%, 3.8%, .19%.

6. Ibid., for source data only, December 31, 1964–December 31, 2014 S&P 500 With Monthly Dividends vs. CD 6-Months With Dividends; 10.28% Average Return vs. 6.68 % Average Return; $10,000=$501,669 in Stocks and $132,634 in CDs.

7. Damodaran, PhD, Aswath. S&P 500, Dividends Not Reinvested, Rolling Averages Calculated by author.

8. Ibid., S&P 500 Dividends Not Reinvested, 3-Month T-Bills, December 31, 1927–December 31, 2014.

9. Ibid., S&P 500 Dividends Not Reinvested, December 31, 1927–December 31, 2014.

10. Ibid.

11. Securities Industry and Financial Markets Association (SIFMA), "Equity and Bond Ownership in America, 2008."

12. American Funds Distributors, Inc., hypothetical illustration.

13. Value Line Publishing, 1992, and Moody's.

14. Shaw, Richard, "Stock Dividend Yields vs. Interest Rates: An 80 Year History," *Seeking Alpha,* September 4, 2007, *http://seekingalpha.com/article/46288-stock-dividend-yields-vs-interest-rates-an-80-year-history.*

15. American Funds Distributors, Inc., hypothetical illustration, 30-Day Money Market Index—All Taxable, Consumer Price Index—U.S., December 1, 2004–November 30, 2014.

16. Damodaran, PhD, Aswath, and U.S. Inflation Calculator, December 31, 1927–December 31, 2014, *www. usinflationcalculator.com.*

17. American Funds Distributors, Inc., hypothetical illustration, DJIA With Monthly Dividends, Treasury Bill—3-Month, December 31, 1933–December 31, 2013.

18. Morningstar, Inc. 15 years through December 31, 2014, Distinct Portfolios.

19. "ICI Study: Mutual Fund–Owning Households' Willingness to Take Investment Risk Remains Subdued," Investment Company Institute, October 31, 2013, *www.ici.org/pressroom/news/13 _ news _ charac _ own.*

20. American Funds Hypothetical, Thomson Reuters, S&P With Monthly Dividends, 30-Day Money Market Index, Best, Median, Worst 10-Year Rolling Periods, December 31, 1975–December 31, 2014.

21. American Funds Hypothetical, Thomson Reuters, 30-Day Money Market Index, 50% S&P 500 With Monthly Dividends, 50% Barclays Capital U.S. Aggregate Index, Best, Median, Worst 10-Year Rolling Periods, December 31, 1975–December 31, 2014.

22. The Federal Reserve Board's Survey of Consumer Finances for 2007, *www.federalreserve.gov/econresdata/scf/scf _ 2007.htm.*

23. Ibid.

24. Personal interview with the author, April 7, 2008, Nashville, Tennessee.

25. Personal e-mail interview with the author. Permission granted to use February 27, 2015.

26. Ivanov, Vladimir, and Scott Bauguess, "Capital Raising in the U.S.: An Analysis of Unregistered Offerings Using the Regulation D Exemption, 2009–2012."

27. Minsky, Hyman P. *The Financial Instability Hypothesis,* The Jerome Levy Economics Institute of Bard College, May 1992.

28. *Wall Street Journal,* Letter to the Editor, 3/28/01.

29. American Funds, Inc. hypothetical, December 31, 1973–December 31, 2013, one-year growth of $10,000.

30. Gnos, Claude, and Louis-Phillipe Rochon, eds. *Post-Keynesian Principles of Economic Policy* (Cheltenham, UK: Edgar Elgar Publishing, 2006), p. 70.

Day 3

1. "Investing in Hell With Chris Davis," Morningstar, Inc., January 23, 2015, *investors.morningstar.com.*

2. Phelps William Lyon. BrainyQuote.com, Xplore Inc, 2015, *www.brainyquote.com/quotes/quotes/w/williamlyo377109. html.*

3. Dewdney, A.K. *200% of Nothing: An Eye-Opening Tour Through the Twists and Turns of Math Abuse and Innumeracy* (New York: Wiley, 1996).

4. Rothman, MD, Russell. "Addressing Health Literacy: Talking Plainly to Improve Patient Care," *Journal of the Royal College of Physicians of Edinburgh 40* 2010:194–5, *www.rcpe.ac.uk/sites/default/files/editorial _ 4.pdf.*

5. Baker, H. Kent, and Victor Ricciardi. "Understanding Behavioral Aspects of Financial Planning and Investing," *Journal of Financial Planning,* March 2015.

6. Morningstar, Inc., September 15, 1997–September 15, 2007, at NAV.

7. Morningstar, Inc. All Large Value and Small Growth Funds With 19-Year Track Records, Annual Returns 10 Years Through June 30, 2013.

8. Baker, Malcolm P., Brendan Bradley, and Jeffrey A. Wurgler, "Benchmarks as Limits to Arbitrage: Understanding the Low Volatility Anomaly," March 2010, NYU Working Paper No. FIN-10-002, *http://ssrn.com/abstract=1585031.*

9. Laise, Eleanor. "Protecting Your Nest Egg in Volatile Times: Today's Retirees Must Control Risk Even as Longer Lifespans Mean They Need More Income," *The Wall Street Journal,* January 16, 2008, p. D1.

10. Ibid., Average Annual Returns.

11. Falkenstein, PhD, Eric G. *The Missing Risk Premium,* 2012.

12. Lauricella, Tom. "Investors Hope the '10s Beat the '00s," *The Wall Street Journal,* December 20, 2009, *http://online. wsj.com/articles/SB10001424052748704786204574607993448 916718.*

13. Israelsen, PhD, Craig. "A Perfect Portfolio," Financial Planning Website, September 1, 2008 *www.financial-planning.com/asset/article/651261/perfect-portfolio. html?pg=.*

14. Baldwin, Amy. "Fund Investors Forsake Buy and Hold Theory," *The Florida Times Union,* February 18, 2001, *http://jacksonville.com/tu-online/stories/021801/ bus _ 5414189.html.*

15. Kessler, Andy. "Say Goodbye To Momentum Investing," *The Wall Street Journal,* December 4, 2000, *www.andykessler. com/andy _ kessler/2000/12/wsj _ say _ goodbye.html.*

16. Loeb, Marshall. "Five Ways to Stay Cool in a Down Market," CBS News Marketwatch, March 20, 2008, *www.cbsnews.com/ news/five-ways-to-stay-cool-in-a-down-market/.*

17. Zweig, Jason. "Why Market Forecasts Keep Missing the Mark," *The Wall Street Journal,* January 24, 2009.

18. Ibid.

19. Hulbert, Mark. "Calling a Stock-Market Top Is Only Half the Battle, Market Timers Who Side-Stepped the 2000–02 Bear Market Aren't Long-Term Winners," *The Wall Street Journal,* August 8, 2014, *http://online.wsj. com/articles/calling-a-stock-market-top-is-only-half-the-battle-1407514856.*

20. Glassman, James K. "Put Your Faith in Ford," *Kiplinger's,* March 2007.

21. Jaffee, Chuck. "You Are Your Portfolio's Worst Enemy," Marketwatch, Inc., August 30, 2014, *www.marketwatch.com/ story/you-are-your-portfolios-worst-enemy-2014-08-25/ print.*

22. Ibid.

23. *From the Earth to the Moon,* HBO Mini-Series, *http:// en.wikipedia.org/wiki/Pete _ Conrad,* and verified by Howard A. Klausner, author of *Rocketman: Astronaut Pete Conrad's Incredible Ride to the Moon and Beyond.*

24. Morningstar, Inc. 10-Year Annual Returns Through October 31, 2010. Average: all mutual funds, minimum 10-year returns, minimum purchase $10,000. Cheapest: same criteria and lowest gross expense ratio.

25. Morningstar Advisor Workstation, hypothetical illustration, December 31, 1993–December 31, 2013, DJIA TR = 10.20%/Yearly vs. Morningstar SEC/Utilities TR (U.S.D, F00000LJ9G) = 7.73%/yearly.

26. Morningstar, Inc., period ending August 31, 2014.

27. Morningstar, Inc. through August 31, 2014, and author's computations. Load of either 4.50% or 4.75% up-front assumed for load funds. All data estimated and not guaranteed. NER = net expense ratio. Past performance is no guarantee of future returns.

28. Morningstar Advisor Workstation, Glossary.

29. "2111. Suitability," *FINRA Manual,* eff. May 1, 2014, *http://finra.complinet.com/en/display/display _ main. html?rbid=2403&element _ id=9859.*

30. "Fiduciary Standard Resource Center," SIFMA.org, *www. sifma.org/issues/private-client/fiduciary-standard/ overview/.*

31. Spencer, Jane. "Lessons from the Brain-Damaged Investor," *The Wall Street Journal,* July 21, 2005.

32. Ibid.

33. Ibid.

34. Ferry, John. "Fiscal Feelings: Behavioral Finance Explains Why We Invest the Way We Do," *Worth,* March 2008, p. 66.

35. Lehrer, Jonah. "Don't! The Secret of Self-Control," *The New Yorker,* May 18, 2009, *www.newyorker.com/ magazine/2009/05/18/dont-2.*

Day 4

1. Newcomer, Mabel. "The Opportunity for College Women in a Democracy," *The Vassar Miscellany* News, October 1935, p. 9.

2. Personal interview with the author, April 7, 2008, Nashville, Tennessee.

3. Conference call with Advisor Products, Inc., February 20, 2009.

4. Snyder, Chris, and Hutch Ashoo. "Investors, Advisers Both Make Mistakes," *Business Wise,* May 9–15, 2008, *www. pillarwm.com/pillar-articles/EBBT-Investors-advisors- mistakes-050908.pdf.*

5. "2003 Quantitative Analysis of Investor Behavior," Dalbar, Inc.; multiple sources.

6. Seawright, Bob, "How Advisors Can Make Better Investing Decisions," *Research Magazine,* May 2014, *www.thinkadvisor.com/2014/04/28/ how-advisors-can-make-better-investing-decisions.*

7. Investment Company Institute through December 31, 2012, and other sources. Average stock and bond fund investor returns. Investor returns represented by change in total mutual fund assets excluding sales, redemptions, and exchanges. Benchmarks: bond funds, Barclay's Aggregate Bond Index; stock funds, S&P 500.

8. Seawright, "How Advisors Can Make."

9. Zuccaro, Robert. *Dow, 30,000 by 2008: Why It's Different This Time* (South Carolina: Booksurge Publishing, 2008); Glassman, James, and Kevin Hassett. *Dow 36,000: The New Strategy for Profiting From the Coming Rise in the Stock Market* (New York: Three Rivers Press, 1999); Elias, David. *Dow 40,000: Strategies for Profiting From the Greatest Bull*

Market in History (New York: McGraw-Hill, 1999); Kadlec, Charles W. *Dow 100,000: Fact or Fiction,* (New Jersey: Prentice Hall Press, 1999); "Dow 1,000,000" is a joke, not unlike the others.

10. Regnier, Pat. "Is it All Over for Stocks?" *Money Magazine,* December 19, 2008.

11. Morningstar Advisor Workstation, hypothetical illustration, December 31, 1979–December 31, 2014, S&P 500 TR (USD), indexes are not investable.

12. Chang, Ellen. "Hussman 80% Chance of Big Market Crash," *StreetTalk,* December 4, 2009.

13. *Dick Davis Digest,* issue unknown.

14. Solomon, Jesse. "Warren Buffett Is Buying Stocks This Week," CNN Money, October 2, 2014, *http://money.cnn.com/2014/10/02/investing/ warren-buffett-buying-the-stock-dip/.*

15. Fink, Jim. "Waiting for QE3 Will Keep Stock Market in Bullish," Copyright 2015 "Investing Daily," a division of Capitol Information Group, Inc. All rights reserved. *www. investingdaily.com/15548/waiting-for-qe3-will-keep-stock-market-in-bullish-trend/,* August 14, 2012.

16. Washington Mutual Investors Fund 2001 Annual Report, *www.sec.gov/Archives/edgar/containers/fix030/104865/0000 104865015000017/n30.*

17. Scholl, Jaye. "Forever Bullish," *Barron's,* October 29, 2001, *http://online.barrons.com/articles/ SB1004143496864011560?tesla=y.*

18. American Funds Distributors, Inc., "Newsline," June 30, 2008, p. 2.

19. Easterling, Ed. Copyright 2014, *www.crestmontresearch.com/ faqs/.*

20. Vanderbilt University Owen Graduate School of Management, *http://owen.vanderbilt.edu/vanderbilt/about/faculty-research/f _ profile.cfm?id=136.*

21. Personal correspondence with the author. Permission granted to use material March 1, 2015.

22. Jaffe, Chuck. "Morningstar Puts Mutual Funds on a Podium," *MarketWatch,* November 20, 2011, *www.marketwatch.com/story/morningstar-puts-mutual-funds-on-a-podium-2011-11-20.*

23. Frank Russell Company.

24. CFA Institute, December 2006. Data from Frank Russell Company and American Funds *Insights,* Fall 2007. Lit No. MFCPWP-011-1007P.

25. SEI, Morningstar Direct, U.S. Large Blend Universe.

26. Keefe, John. "Performance Anxiety?" *PlanSponsor Magazine,* May 17, 2010, *www.plansponsor.com/MagazineArticle.aspx?id=6442459486.*

27. Baker, H. Kent, and Victor Ricciardi. "How Biases Affect Investor Behaviour," *The European Financial Review,* February–March 2014, *http://papers.ssrn.com/sol3/papers.cfm?abstract _ id=2457425.*

28. Ibid.

29. Saad, Lydia. "U.S. Stock Ownership Stays at Record Low," Gallup, Inc., copyright 2015. All rights reserved. Results for this Gallup poll are based on telephone interviews conducted April 4–14, 2013, with a random sample of 2,017 adults, aged 18 and older, living in all 50 U.S. states and the District of Columbia. For results based on the total sample of national adults, one can say with 95% confidence that the maximum margin of sampling error is ±3 percentage points. This graph is an interpretation of data compiled by Gallup, Inc. However, Gallup, Inc. had no part in the creation of this graphic interpretation, *www.gallup.com/poll/162353/stock-ownership-stays-record-low.aspx,* May 8, 2013.

30. S&P 500 December 31, 2007–December 31, 2013; and Saad, Lydia, "U.S. Stock Ownership Stays at Record Low," Gallup poll, May 8, 2013.

31. Ludwig, Olivier. "S&P: 1% Of Active Large-Cap Funds Reliably Beat Market," ETF.com, June 9, 2011, *www.etf.com/ sections/features/9362-sap-few-active-funds-retain-their-edge.html.*

32. Standard & Poor's. All periods as of March for each year. Past performance does not guarantee future results.

33. Rawson, CFA, Michael, "Fund Flows Not Always Written in the Stars," Morningstar, Inc., May 14, 2014, *www. morningstar.com/cover/videocenter.aspx?id=647960.*

34. Ramin, Joel. "Interview With Paul Tudor Jones II (Abridged)," January 13, 2000, *http://chinese-school. netfirms.com/Paul-Tudor-Jones-interview.html.*

35. Reed, Stanley. "UBS Gets Whacked by Subprime Mess," *Business Week,* October 1, 2007, *www.businessweek. com/stories/2007-10-01/ubs-gets-whacked-by-subprime-messbusinessweek-business-news-stock-market-and-financial-advice.*

36. Portnoy, Brian, PhD, CFA. *The Investor's Paradox: The Power of Simplicity in a World of Overwhelming Choice* (New York: Palgrave Macmillan Trade, 2014).

37. ICI Annual Mutual Fund Shareholder Trackign Survey, Federal Reserve Board of Consumer Finances (SCF), and Standard & Poor's.

Day 5

1. "In-Flight Surgery Improvised," *Deseret News*, May 23, 1995, *www.deseretnews.com/article/460423/IN-FLIGHT-SURGERY-IMPROVISED.html?pg=all.*

2. Trottman, Melanie, and Stephanie Chen. "In Death's Wake, Questions About In-Flight Aid," *The Wall Street*

Journal, February 26, 2008, *http://online.wsj.com/articles/ SB12039873786979222392/26/08.*

3. Hamilton, Josh, P. "Buying What Buffett Buys on Filings Doubles S&P 500 (Update 1)," *Bloomberg, LP,* November 16, 2007, *www.bloomberg.com/apps/news?pid=newsarchive&sid =aHszGRaHR1M4.*

4. Sandberg, Jared. "Shooting Messengers Makes Us Feel Better but Work Dumber," *The Wall Street Journal,* September 11, 2007, p. B1, *http://online.wsj.com/article/ SB118945866345322967.html.*

5. Baker and Ricciardi, "How Biases Affect."

6. Baker and Ricciardi, "Understanding Behavioral Aspects."

7. Ibid.

8. Hollis, Mark David, and Timothy Alan Friese-Greene. *Living in Another World* (Universal Music Publishing Group).

9. Healthline Networks, Inc. and Marketdata Enterprises, Inc.

10. "Study Shows Health Coaches Effective in Helping People Lose Weight, Live Healthier Lives," *The American Council on Exercise CertifiedNews,* October 2012, *www.acefitness.org/certifiednewsarticle/2892/ study-shows-health-coaches-effective-in-helping/.*

11. Ibid.

12. Personal interview with the author, April 7, 2008, Nashville, Tennessee.

13. Schiff, Lewis. "7 Habits of the Ultra Wealthy," Yahoo! Small Business Advisor, March 22, 2013, *https://smallbusiness. yahoo.com/advisor/7-habits-of-the-ultra-wealthy-181131868. html.*

14. Mitchell, Josh. "About Half of Kids With Single Moms Live in Poverty," *The Wall Street Journal,* November 25, 2013, *http://blogs.wsj.com/economics/2013/11/25/ about-half-of-kids-with-single-moms-live-in-poverty/.*

15. Quinlan, Adriane. "Average U.S. Family Lost One Third of its Net Worth in Past Decade, Study Reports, NOLA.com, *The Times-Picayune,* July 29, 2014, *www.nola.com/politics/index.ssf/2014/07/poor _ have _ doubled _ debt _ average.html.*

16. U.S. Securities and Exchange Commission, "Affinity Fraud: How to Avoid Investment Scams That Target Groups," *www.sec.gov/investor/pubs/affinity.htm.*

17. Zweig, Jason, "How Bernie Madoff Made Smart Folks Look Dumb," *The Wall Street Journal,* December 13, 2008, *http://online.wsj.com/article/SB1229122663389002855.html?mod=article-outset-box.*

18. Ibid.

19. Ibid.

20. Tergesen, Anne. "Your 401(k) Plan's Secret Weapon," *Marketwatch Encore,* May 13, 2014, *http://blogs.marketwatch.com/encore/2014/05/13/your-401k-plans-secret-weapon/;* AON Hewitt full study: "Help in Defined Contribution Plans: 2006 through 2012," 2014, *http://corp.financialengines.com/employers/FinancialEngines-2014-Help-Report.pdf.*

21 AIG Financial Advisors, 2003.

22. "ICI Research Perspective," *ICI Research Perspective Vol. 19, No. 2,* February 2013, *www.ici.org/pdf/per19-02.pdf.*

23. Saad, Lydia. "U.S. Investors Opt for Human Over Online Financial Advice," Gallup, Inc., August 15, 2014.

24. Ibid.

25. Zweig, Jason. "Financial Advisers: Show Us Your Numbers," *The Wall Street Journal,* July 11, 2014, *http://blogs.wsj.com/moneybeat/2014/07/11/financial-advisers-show-us-your-numbers/.*

26. Prince and Associates marketing collateral.

Day 6

1. Dimensional Website, *us.dimensional.com/philosophy/ diversification.aspx*.

2. "What's Your Investment Philosophy?" Key Financial Solutions LLC Website blog post, November 5, 2012, *www. keyfeeonly.com/tag/diversification*.

3. Murray, Alan, "Cuban on Investing: Diversification Is for Idiots," *WSJ.com, YouTube*, August 12, 2011, *www.youtube. com/watch?v=u5Pp1HEKSPM*.

4. Morningstar, Inc., August 31, 1976–August 31, 2014. 100% Stocks: Vanguard 500 Index; Balanced: Vanguard Wellington Fund. Worst one, three, and 10 years are not calendar years. Past performance is no guarantee of future returns. Please read a prospectus before making an investment.

5. **Stocks:** Bloomberg, August 27, 2014, *http:bloom.bg/1nB2Jcx*. **Bonds:** 3Twelve Total World Bond™, December 30, 2013, *http://bit.ly/1hZjyzc*. **Real Estate:** Savills Word Research/ Wealth-X, January 2014, *http://bit.ly/1dXeHrt*. **Commodities:** Gross, not notional values, BIS, December 2013, *bit. ly/1C2jOWD*. **Cash:** Taxable and Tax-Free Money Markets, January 2014, *www.imoneynet.com/*. All figures approximate.

6. **U.S. Stocks:** S&P 500 Composite Total Return December 31, 1969–December 31, 2014, Thomson Reuters Investment View. **Non–U.S. Stocks:** MSCI EAFE GR U.S.D December 31, 1969–December 31, 2014, Morningstar Advisor Workstation. **U.S. Bonds:** U.S. Treasury 10-year bond at end of each year from the Federal Reserve of St. Louis (FRED) 1970–1975, Aswath Damodaran. Barclays U.S. Agg. Bond TR USD (U.S.D)(IDX) December 31, 1975–December 31, 2014, Morningstar Advisor Workstation. **Non–U.S. Bonds:** December 31, 1969–December 31, 1980: Roger G. Ibbotson, Richard C. Carr, and Anthony W. Robinson, *Financial Analysts Journal Vol. 38, No. 4* (July–August 1982): 61–83, Published by CFA Institute, article stable URL [*www.jstor.*

org/stable/4478566, Citigroup World Government Index December 31, 1980–December 31, 2014, American Funds Hypothetical. **Cash:** 3-Month Treasury Bill: Secondary Market Rate from the Board of Governors of the Federal Reserve System December 31, 1969–December 31, 2014, *http://bit. ly/1mvkVWQ.* **Real Estate:** *7Twelve 2013 Research Report* by Craig Israelsen January 2013, p. 53, NAREIT Index 1970– 1977 (annual returns for 1970 and 1971 were regression-based estimates inasmuch as the NAREIT Index did not provide annual returns until 1972), Dow Jones U.S. Select REIT Index December 31, 1977–December 31, 2014 Morningstar Advisor Workstation. **Commodities:** S&P GSCI Index December 31, 1969–December 31,2014, Thomson Reuters Investment View.

7. Conference call, Advisor Products, Inc.

8. *D&B U.S. Business Trends Report,* October 2010, Copyright 2010 Dun & Bradstreet, *http://dnb.com.au/library/scripts/ objectifyMedia.aspx?file=pdf/48/70.pdf&siteID=1&str _ title=Full%20report.pdf.*

9. Charan, Ram, and Jerry Useem. "Why Companies Fail: CEOs Offer Every Excuse but the Right One: Their Own Errors. Here Are Ten Mistakes to Avoid," *Fortune Magazine,* May 15, 2002, *http://archive.fortune.com/magazines/ fortune/fortune _ archive/2002/05/27/323712/index.htm.*

10. Prudential Insurance seminar attended by author, December 1, 2009, Nashville, Tennessee.

11. Sastry, Keertana. "From Bank to Broke: 20 Celebs Who TANKED Their Fortunes," *Business Insider,* May 11, 2012, *www.businessinsider.com/from-bank-to-broke-here-are-20- celebs-who-went-bankrupt-2012-5?op=1#ixzz3Nrz001sy.*

12. Morningstar, Inc.

13. See Day 6, note #6 for a list of each of the indexes of the Diversified Portfolio.

14. Ibid.

15. Derman, Emanuel. "Finance by the Numbers," *The Wall Street Journal,* August 22, 2007, *http://online.wsj.com/articles/SB118774956064304935.*

16. Laise, "Protecting Your Nest Egg."

17. Source data from Craig Israelsen, PhD.

18. Personal correspondence with the author.

19. Burnside, Daniel J. "How Many Stocks Do You Need to Be Diversified?" *AAII Journal* (July 2004), *www.aaii.com/journal/article/how-many-stocks-do-you-need-to-be-diversified-.touch.*

20. Eaglesham, Jean, Katy Burne, and Justin Baer. "Finra Scrutinizes Banks' Role in Bond Market," *The Wall Street Journal,* April 10, 2014, *http://on.wsj.com/QlpN52.*

21. Personal conversation with the author, 1995, San Diego, California.

22. ETFS/Funds from the 3Twelve™ Total Bond barometer chart, AGZ: iShares Barclays Agency Bond Fund, BKLN: PowerShares Senior Loan Portfolio, BWZ: SPDR Barclays Capital Short Term International Treasury, CFT: iShares Barclays Credit Bond Fd, CWB: SPDR Barclays Capital Convertible Bond, EMB: iShares JP Morgan Em Bond Fd, FMPXX: Fidelity Instit Money Market Fd, IEF: iShares Barclays 7–10 Year Treasury Bond Fd, JNK: SPDR® Barclays High Yield Bond, PICB: PowerShares International Corporate Bond Portfolio, VTIP: Vanguard Short-Term Inflation-Protected Securities, VFIJX: Vanguard GNMA Fund Admiral Shares. Source data: Morningstar Inc., December 31, 2013 through December 31, 2014. Past performance is no guarantee of future returns. Diversification does not guarantee a profit or protect against loss. These appear for illustration purposes only, and are not a solicitation or recommendation for these or any other securities.

23 "Correlation Explained [TimeWeb]," *Biz/ed,* November 2, 2002, *www.bized.co.uk/timeweb/crunching/crunch _ relate _ expl.htm.*

24. Martin, Andrew D. "Must Bond Investors Fear Rising Interest Rates?" *Advisor Perspectives,* January 24, 2012, *www.advisorperspectives.com/newsletters12/Must _ Bond _ Investors _ Fear _ Rising _ Interest _ Rates. php* AND Martin, Andrew D., "Bursting the Bond Bubble Babble," *Advisor Perspectives,* June 11, 2013, *www. advisorperspectives.com/newsletters13/pdfs/Bursting _ the _ Bond _ Bubble _ Babble.pdf.*

25. Browne, Christopher H., et al. "Ten Ways to Beat an Index," *https://thetaoofwealth.foles.wordpress.com/2013/10-ways-to-beat-an-index.pdf,* p. 3.

26. Ibid.

27. Morningstar Advisor Workstation, hypothetical illustration, five years ending 2008 = –1.94%, Large Blend, 474 distinct portfolios; five years ending 2008 = –1.05%, Large Value, 333 distinct portfolios; S&P 500 –2.19%.

28. Bergmann, Andrew. "World's Largest Economies," CNN Money, *http://money.cnn.com/news/economy/ world _ economies _ gdp/.*

29. Speech at the Exchange Club of Nashville (now the Economic Club of Nashville), November 18, 2008.

30. "President Ronald Reagan—On the Challenger Disaster," The History Place™ Great Speeches Collection, January 28, 1986, *www.historyplace.com/speeches/reagan-challenger.htm.*

31. Mallory, Simon. "Lawmakers Frustrated with Obama Administration's Oil Spill Response, CNN.com, May 26, 2010, *www.cnn.com/2010/POLITICS/05/26/lawmakers.oil.spill./*

32. "Remarks by the President to the Nation on the BP Oil Spill," The White House Office of the Press Secretary, June 15, 2010, *www.whitehouse.gov/the-press-office/ remarks-president-nation-bp-oil-spill.*

Epilogue

1. "Money Can Buy Happiness," *The Economist*, May 2, 2013, *www.economist.com/blogs/graphicdetail/2013/05/daily-chart-0*.

2. Taylor, III, Alex. "Still Smokin'," *Fortune Magazine*, June 15, 2006, *http://archive.fortune.com/2006/06/13/magazines/fortune/iacocca _ retirementguide _ fortune/index.htm*.

3. Israelsen, PhD, Craig. "Family Financial Stewardship," Mission Fund Prep Website, *http://missionfundprep.org/index.php/articles/parents-of-youth?view=kb&kbartid=7&tmpl=component*.

Publishing a book is a team sport. My friends, family, and business associates encouraged, supported, read early versions, and plucked the book's errant feathers. I have a long list of acknowledgments because I believe the first commandment is to be grateful.

Thank you Stephanie Martin, my wife, for abiding early mornings of writing and endless conversations of a style and grammatical sort. I most appreciate your sharing in all the little victories and defeats that turn a few ideas into a book.

Thanks to my father, Jim Martin, who has always been the sturdier writer and reader. His idea to write in a more active voice and keep it simple helped you, reader, enjoy the book more. Thank you JoAnne Martin for adding a steady, thoughtful, and human voice to our family. Thanks to my living brothers, David and Peter, and deceased brother, Chris. No one could have taught me better the science of risk management.

The best relationship I have had in the securities business has been with Girard Securities (and its predecessor firms, Sentra and Spelman). Thank you Richard P. (Dick) Woltman. And thanks to Jason Rogers—the best friend a guy can have in this business. Jason never runs out of good ideas and is willing to kick some ankles if someone tries to push around one of his reps. The entire staff at Girard I greet with hugs: Cheryl Appleby, Dominick Zizzo, Jacklyn McCray, Patti Kuhlman, John Barragan, and many others. And I am *not* a hugger. They are the first family in the investment industry. Special thanks for Bonnie Wusz, a CFP in Orange, California, a perennial Girard top producer, and a true professional. She read my manuscript with great care and gave me great advice, which I incorporated into the final draft.

Thank you to my Girard clients—for confidentiality sake I can't name you! But, see if you fit this description: You have been with me many years, you have suffered through my bad ideas, and the occasional good ones, you have waited patiently for me to return your phone call, and you put up with my changing firms five times in the last 30 years. I may as well have called you by name.

Thank you to my partners at 7Twelve Advisors, LLC. Ben Doochin, Chris Radford, Rob and Alex Blagojevich, Jim Hunt, Steve Eisen, Brent Goers, Clark Liddell, and Craig Israelsen make doing the hardest thing you can do in the investment business—building product—a joy.

My thanks to the pantheon of talent who wrote endorsements for *Dollarlogic*. The list is a who's who of notables in the investment industry: Susie Woltman Tietjen, Jack Tierney, Bob Huebscher, Fritz Meyer, Norb Vonnegut, Ron Delegge, Eric Falkenstein, and PhD, Victor Ricciardi.

Special thanks to Dr. Art Laffer, who wrote the Foreword. There is nothing dismal about the science that Dr. Laffer promulgates. I have been a fan of his since I studied economics in the 1980s. No economist has a clearer and more accurate vision of what blesses and befalls our material life. The Laffer Curve is one of the very few economic theories that knows no boundaries; it works in every developed nation. This fact is what demolishes his critics.

Thank you to my business coach, Dan Haile of Haile Coaching & Leadership, who has taught me that the answer is usually be respectful, be firm, be yourself. And thank you to Seawell Brandau, who mentored out of me many a bad habit.

Thank you to Dr. Aswath Damodaran at Stern School of Business at New York University. Dr. Damodaran provides for free (just because he's a great guy and loves this stuff) endless custom market data at *damodaran.com.* He is a legend in finance, as evidenced by his Twitter followers—all of us market data nerds. He has also responded quickly to various questions I have had over e-mail, all the time likely wondering *Who the hell is this guy Martin who keeps e-mailing me?* I am a proud disciple of Dr. Damodaran's cult.

My thanks to Gemini Fund Services and the Northern Lights Variable Trust, Andrew Rogers, Eddie Lund, and Tony Hertl, for taking a flyer on us and being at the vanguard of the alternative fund space. And thank you David Jurczak, for being the hardest-working wholesaler in the industry.

Many thanks to these industry people who helped us turn a pie chart into a mutual fund: Erik Ambrose with WallachBeth—truly one of the great guys in our business; Michael Cafiero at Cantor Fitzgerald; St. Bryce Kurfees; Ron Harkey, industry giant and wonderful human being; JoAnn

Strasser, vice chair of corporate transactions and securities at Thompson Hine; Chris Winn of AdvisorAssist; Lori Powell of Nationwide; Ann Raible of Jefferson National; and Michael Reidy of Security Benefit.

Special thanks to Craig Israelsen, PhD. Craig is the most important figure in the investment industry today. There, I said it. His 7Twelve™ model's utility is matched only by its elegance. And he has a remarkable "open source" attitude. That is, he has taught a generation of advisors to cooperate rather than compete with one another. This is better for the client, and the industry, and a better safeguard for the soul.

Thanks to the 800-pound gorilla, otherwise known as AXA. I have never seen such a big company display as much creativity and flexibility as does AXA Advisors and AXA Funds Management Group. Nor have I ever seen a harder-working sales force. Thank you Steve Joenk, Ken Kozlowski, Mike McCarthy, Graham Day, Michael Schumacher, Steve Mabry, Jack Schilt, Scott Hart, and the unstoppable John "Dartman" Wadsworth (to whom I have entrusted my family's future). And thanks to the real workers, the road warriors of our industry: AXA wholesalers Steve Junge, Fran Doherty, Bob Stansbury, Tom Mocogni, Andy Wohl, and too many others to name. I love you guys. Wholesalers teach us advisors everything we need to know.

Thank you Nationwide Financial, Security Benefit, and Jefferson National—leaders in the financial products industry. Nationwide basically invented the multi-manager in one package approach, and Security Benefit, Jefferson National, and Nationwide have perfected it.

Thank you Todd Colburn, who for many years was my business partner and a ton of fun to work with. Many ideas and philosophies you read here are things we kicked around while playing office handball in the stairwell, or while passing the football in our coats and ties in downtown Nashville traffic while everyone else worked.

Thank you to Ryan Bartlett with Goldman Sachs in NYC. Ryan is a true gentleman, is an early supporter of 7Twelve, and can fly at any altitude.

Many thanks to the always helpful and encouraging Kyle Roy—the world's only wholesaler who has his own custom 800 number.

After 30 years in the investment business I am sentimental. My start was with Merrill Lynch in Nashville and Manhattan. Those who always made time for my tiresome questions were Andy Spurgeon, Bill Turner, Jim Humphreys, Andy Valentine, Lewis Thompson, Morris Early, Jorge Arias (NYC), Frank Collins (NYC) who first hired me; and Sue Estep, Trish Koller, Peggy Downey, Brenda Jones, and the rest of the *girls* (among whom I was the only male) in operations. The girls showed me how unimportant I was and killed the little brat in me with charm and humor—a sober start in a great industry. Thank you.

My first love is literature, though you may find little evidence of that in this book. I am grateful to these hallowed professors at Vanderbilt University who taught me how to read, write, and, most of all, think: Edward Friedman, PhD, Roy Gottfried, PhD, Mark Jarman, PhD, Frank Wcislo, PhD, Chris Hassel, PhD, Leah Marcus, PhD, and John Lachs, PhD.

Thank you to Dr. Wayne and Dr. Faye Robbins—the smartest, most virtuous couple I know. Dr. Wayne Robbins was the founder of the Cockroft Forum for Free Enterprise— the most successful university-based free-enterprise executive forum in the country. And Faye is the unique historian who brings wisdom to dates and facts. I will always cherish how you two believed in me far ahead of my readiness for such trust. God bless you both.

Thank you to my assistants who helped work on this book while performing many additional research duties, especially Sophie Gao, Dalton Easterwood, and Jimmy Feeman. If you are down on Millennials or Generation Z, then you have not hired one. The world has a bright future if it is one day populated with Sophies, Daltons, and Jimmys.

Many thanks to Career Press. You have hit on a great formula and are bunch of pros. Thank you for that *Young Frankenstein* Gene Wilder movie moment when you looked up from the pages of my manuscript with insanity in your eyes and shouted, "It...could...work!" Thank you Michael Pye, Laurie Kelly-Pye, Adam Schwartz, Jodi Brandon (the fastest editor I have ever worked with), Jeff Piasky, Kirsten Dalley, Gina Schenck, and Nate Ohl.

Thank you to Christina Verigan for taking my jumbled box of words and pictures and turning it into something that a publisher can read.

Salute to Rob Blagojevich—the toughest guy I know and my best friend. Always encouraging, always positive. Read his spectacular book, *Fundraiser A: My Fight for Freedom and Justice.*

Finally, thank you very much to Debby Englander. The only reason her name appears at the end of these acknowledgments instead of the very beginning is that I am married. Debby has put up with me since 2007. Had I not met her, this book would not exist. She is a former senior editor with Wiley and is now a publishing consultant. She introduced me, thankfully, to Christina Verigan, who translated *Dollarlogic* to publishing-speak and introduced me to many publishers, including the fine people at Career Press.